Waiting to Conceive

A Devotional for Women Seeking Motherhood

WESTBOW
PRESS
A DIVISION OF THOMAS NELSON
& ZONDERVAN

Scripture taken from the King James Version of the Bible.

Scripture taken from the New King James Version. Copyright 1979, 1980,
1982 by Thomas Nelson, inc. Used by permission. All rights reserved.

WestBow Press books may be ordered through booksellers or by contacting:

WestBow Press
A Division of Thomas Nelson & Zondervan
1663 Liberty Drive
Bloomington, IN 47403
www.westbowpress.com
1 (866) 928-1240

ISBN: 978-1-4908-5748-0 (sc)
ISBN: 978-1-4908-5749-7 (hc)
ISBN: 978-1-4908-5750-3 (e)

Library of Congress Control Number: 2014918900

Printed in the United States of America.

WestBow Press rev. date: 11/5/2014

Dedication

To every woman who yearns to be a mother, To all who know someone seeking the joy of becoming a mum, And to the Almighty God for inspiring this work.

Contents

Foreword

When I heard Sophia Loren's story, it touched me deeply. She was a world-renowned actress and classic beauty with everything she could dream of: a loving husband, more money than she could ever hope for, and the world at her feet. Yet, she had no child. Her attempts at producing offspring were met with failure more than once, and she was devastated. Each time, she lost the pregnancy around three months, and she was beside herself with despair. Then her doctor suggested a radical approach – bed rest for the full nine months! Her husband couldn't imagine it, but she was keen. So Sophia Loren disappeared from public life during this pregnancy. Away from the glare of prying eyes and razor-sharp tongues, she rested and read, probably praying and meditating. Her pregnancy prospered, and she gave birth to her first child after years of trying.

This story resonates with millions of women the world over. The desire to have a child is the deepest need in many women – everything else pales into insignificance if this is not fulfilled. Even more devastating is when a woman miscarries. The pain is indescribable, and the well-meaning words, "You will have another baby," seem insensitive and unfeeling.

I know because I went through it. I was childless for fifteen years and had several miscarriages during that time. I did not wear my need as a garment, but it was a constant yearning I had to fulfil. Looking back, I realised that even though there is no shortcut, it helps when you have the support you need on this journey. I have written this book as support for women who are going through the same journey and need all the help they can get.

I pray it will help you and that you will receive your heart's desire – your own child.

Yinka Ayeni
30th September 2014

Introduction

Childlessness is a part of life and society. There always have been, are now, and always will be many who are childless. Indeed, the first book of the Bible records that the patriarch of faith, Abraham, and his wife, Sarah, faced several years of trials and frustration in waiting for their precious gift – Isaac – to arrive.

Childlessness is no respecter of persons. The rich and poor, young and old from all walks of life face this challenge. It is therefore more common than many people imagine.

This book is for any woman who wants reassurance that she is not alone. Use it as a daily devotional on this journey of discovery and prayerfully read it for divine assistance. This book features scripture and prayer resources to meditate on for fifty-two weeks. It also contains helpful, practical information and advice. There are prayer points that you can use as guidelines for spiritual support. Each week includes a page for you to write down your thoughts, dreams, and prayers. This can be saved as a keepsake – a record of your incredible journey to victory. Some prayers are repeated in certain weeks for emphasis on that particular session.

Acknowledgements

Several people who have helped me in bringing this dream to reality are mentioned here because without them, this work would not have been possible.

I thank God for my parents, who conceived me – Vice Admiral Akintunde Aduwo (NN Retd) and the late Chief Mrs Beki Aduwo. Without them, I would not be present; I thank God for His mercies upon them.

Pastor and Pastor (Mrs) E. A. Adeboye, who have held my hand throughout my challenging battles in life and have never reneged in their love and care. I salute you Sir and Ma and thank God for you both daily. I am keying into your vision of the Maternity and Healthcare Centre on Redemption Camp and extending it into the challenge of childlessness (Enoch Adeboye, Father of Nations, pg 236)

Pastor & Pastor (Mrs) Kolawole, whose prayers have been continuous for my family. I give God the glory for your lives.

Pastor and Mrs Joe Olaiya, who supported my husband and me in prayers over and over. God will not forget your labour of love over us.

To several other Ministers of God who have prayed and trusted God for us, I am eternally grateful. Due to space constraints, I am unable to mention all but the Most High God will reward your labour of love for us.

Thanks to the Croydon Tabernacle members who prayed and believed with me to the end. God will honour you above your fellows.

To Funmi, Mausi, Kingsley and Bolanle, who helped me edit and critique my work – may your crown shine bright among your colleagues.

Thanks to the ladies who have shared their testimonies for the benefit of others – I pray that the joy you are sowing will reap an overflow of joy in your lives,

To Doctors Kola Orimoloye, Yemi Onabowale, Sola Adeaga and Karen, who were pivotal in my journey; I remember Sola coming to my home at 2 am once, when I had a horrible miscarriage: may God promote you all beyond your understanding.

To my husband, Ayomikun, and my son, Folu Oluwasegun, I thank God for you both every day, and I love you. I consider it a privilege from God to be a member of our family and for giving us a testimony He has stood by to defend.

To God: my Saviour, my Father, my Friend, my Mentor, my Shepherd, my Great Encourager, and the One who has never stopped believing in me – even at my lowest depth. I worship and honour You, and I pray that I will always do You proud. Thank You for never letting me go.

Endorsement

This book has at its core the heart cry of someone who waited on the Lord for fifteen years and was not disappointed by the Creator of life. It is an encouraging and comforting resource for those waiting on the Lord to conceive, and it should be approached with much prayer and faith. Remember – Jesus Christ is the same yesterday, today, and forever (Heb. 13: 8). Read this book and receive your miracles, signs, and wonders to the point of overflowing. God bless you.

Pastor (Mrs) Folu Adeboye
Mother-in-Israel (RCCG Worldwide)

Sing

A grateful attitude will go a long way towards receiving good things from the One who made heaven and earth. African dance is very energetic and the women know how to wiggle their abdomen - where a child would be formed, quite vigorously. As an act of faith, I did this and sang praises to the Lord while waiting. Singing is not just an act of worship but a sister to laughter which releases endorphins, keeping you in a healthy state of mind. Counting your blessings also helps keep things in perspective and prevents your life from being ruled by bitterness, frustration, and anger if your blessing of a child is delayed. Start with the end in mind. There is help at hand, and there is a solution somewhere, waiting for you. Your mission is to find it.

Monday: Exod. 15: 1–21

My Insight: When you praise God in advance, the results you desire come alive by faith.

Tuesday: Ps. 144: 1–15

My Insight: While we praise Him, God trains us for the battle of prayer.

Wednesday: Ps. 103: 1–22

My Insight: Praise cannot be a half-hearted exercise. It must be done with our whole heart – intensely and passionately.

Thursday: Ps. 105: 1–45

My Insight: Telling people about the goodness of God is a good habit to form. Simply look around you, see His great goodness, and talk about it.

Friday: 2 Sam. 6: 1–23

My Insight: There is a link between praise and a peaceful pregnancy.

Saturday: Ps. 89:1–52

My Insight: Praise expresses a love affair with God.

Sunday: Acts16: 16–40

My Insight: The physical prison doors opened when Paul and Silas praised God at midnight. Learn how to praise Him in your situations, when everything appears dark and confusing. He can make a way where there seems to be no way.

Fact: A greater percentage of the world's population than you might think is on the same journey as you. For example, infertility affects one in seven couples in the United Kingdom.

Prayer Point:

O Lord, arise and guide me through this journey with grace, peace, and ease, in Jesus' name.

O God, arise and give me the safety and joy I expect, in Jesus' name.

Key Thought: Sing unto the Lord a new song. He has done marvellous things.

Date:

Note / Prayers:

_____

_____

_____

_____

_____

_____

_____

_____

_____

_____

_____

_____

_____

_____

_____

_____

_____

In the Beginning

Waiting on the Lord for anything tests your inner reserves and makes you examine what you believe. The quest for offspring can lead even those who are not believers to a search for the Creator of life. For those who do believe, it tests whether your words of faith in Him are true. Even though the experience is very unpleasant at the time, we will emerge stronger and more purposeful in our approach to life and its many challenges. I believe that the reason I advocate for women's rights to have children without waiting for years and years and for reducing the rate of miscarriage is because of the trials I had in conceiving. If I hadn't been through it myself, I probably would not have written this book.

Monday: Neh. 1: 1–2: 8

My Insight: All things can be aided through fasting and prayer.

Tuesday: Esther 4: 1–5: 4

My Insight: Corporate fasting and prayer makes a way where there seems to be none.

Wednesday: Dan. 1:5–19

My Insight: Fasting can set you apart for great accomplishments.

Thursday: Matt. 4: 1–11

My Insight: Fasting helps you deal with any weaknesses that would want to take your focus off your goal.

Friday: Matt. 6: 5–18

My Insight: Learn how to pray God's way.

Saturday: 1 Kgs. 19: 1–21

My Insight: Never, ever give up! Help is closer than you think.

Sunday: Acts 13: 1–12

My Insight: Fasting and prayer allows the Holy Spirit to empower you and have his way.

Take Note: According to the National Institute of Conception and Embryology (NICE) UK, infertility is defined as the inability to fall pregnant after two years of regular unprotected sex.

Prayer Point:

- Open my eyes, O Lord, to see where my problem is rooted, in Jesus' name (IJN)
- I receive the divine mandate to enforce my right of conception, IJN

Key Thought: The trial of our faith produces patience. See James 1: 3.

Date:

Note / Prayers:

Michelle gave me a
word that next year
at this time I will
be looking at my
babies clothes on the
line and I feel like
Sarah's story completely
encouraged me in this.

Sarah, Hannah, Elizabeth, and I (SHEI)

Three women of the Bible stand out as experiencing what the Creator can do to provide a child – Sarah at ninety years of age (don't try this at home!), Hannah after many years of sorrow, and Elizabeth when she was so far into menopause that her husband was preparing to die childless. Their impossible situations became the fertile ground for miracles of conception when the Creator stepped in. There was an undisputed change in each of their situations. Ask the Lord to show up in your situation as well and to turn it into a victory.

Monday: Gen. 18: 9–15, 21: 1–8

My Insight: God keeps His promises. What has He promised you regarding your offspring?

Tuesday: 1 Sam. 1: 1–28

My Insight: In her desperation, Hannah got her miracle when she dedicated her child, Samuel, to God's purpose – he was to serve God as a priest, for the rest of his life. What is God's purpose for the child or children you are asking Him for?

Wednesday: Luke 1: 5–25

My Insight: John's purpose was stated in verses 15 through 17.

Thursday: Gen. 29: 31–30: 24

My Insight: When Leah switched from competing to praising, she bore a son who was the forerunner of Jesus. Are you quarrelling, angry, bitter, or frustrated? Switch to praise, and see what the Lord will do.

Friday: Judg. 13: 1–24

My Insight: Samson's purpose is stated here.

Saturday: 2 Kgs. 4: 8–37

My Insight: The determination and steadfastness of a mother-to-be can put pressure on heaven to deliver the desired results. Refuse to give up.

Sunday: 1 Sam. 2: 1–19

My Insight: When a dream becomes reality, a song that you never knew you could sing flows from your heart. Hannah's song was deep, inspired, and joyful. So will yours be, in Jesus' name.

Prayer Point:

O Lord, let my testimony at the end of this journey be astonishing.

O Lord, cause me to conceive and to bring forth at the end my own child, in Jesus' name.

Take Note: In the UK, 84 per cent of women fall pregnant within a year of having regular unprotected sex.

Key Thought: "When I cry unto thee, then shall mine enemies turn back: this I know; for God is for me" (Ps. 56: 8–9 KJV).

Date:

Note / Prayers:

_____

_____

_____

_____

_____

_____

_____

_____

_____

_____

_____

_____

_____

_____

_____

_____

Testimonies Can Work a Miracle, Part 1

The purpose of a testimony is to glorify the one who made it possible and to encourage those in a similar condition. It uplifts faith and allows a glimpse of what is to come. The testimony of a lady who brought her baby to a pregnant ladies' fellowship I attended really got me going. She danced vigorously to the front of the room to share her experiences. She had a tough time conceiving and went through a very difficult pregnancy, and God proved Himself to her. This woman's joy was contagious. During the prayer time, I said in my heart, "Lord, I want to give my testimony like this next year." At the time, believing God for this to happen seemed like a near impossibility. I had just had a miscarriage, and this prayer was a deep comfort and inspiration for me.

The words to the song the woman sang haunted me for a long time: "Come and see what the Lord has done ..." Everyone at the meeting saw what the Lord had done, and I was really moved. It spurred me on to keep praying until I had my own child.

Monday: 2 Kgs. 5: 1–19

My Insight: You may get a testimony by humbling yourself to follow simple instructions from the Lord or His servant.

Tuesday: Neh. 1: 1–11

My Insight: Supplication and repentance for the past may be necessary steps to obtaining your testimony. Review your family history for clues regarding what to pray, and ask the Lord's forgiveness for ancestral sins against Him.

Wednesday: Esther 4: 1–17, 5: 1–3

My Insight: You may need to enact corporate fasting and prayer to accomplish your miracle that provides a testimony. Look around for people you can trust, and then join with them to fast and pray for your breakthrough.

Thursday: Ruth 1: 16–18, 3: 9–18

My Insight: Counsel from someone older (spiritually or physically) can go a long way to fast-tracking your miracle. Be discerning in your search for the right person – ask the Lord to guide you.

Friday: Josh. 2: 1–24, 6: 21–25

My Insight: The person who can help you on the journey towards your testimony may be the most unlikely candidate. Be alert and discerning.

Saturday: Matt. 14: 14–21

My Insight: Your miracle may be already present with you – your faith, your money, your tenacity – these are all things God can multiply for your miracle, just as the five loaves and two fishes fed five thousand.

Sunday: Matt. 14: 22–30, 15: 32–38

My Insight: Your faith must hold strong in the face of fear. You may need a second touch from God to strengthen your testimony.

Prayer Point:

Lord, correct any abnormality in my organs used for conception, by your power, IJN.

Let every negative medical report be reversed by the hand of God, IJN.

Fact: During a woman's monthly cycle, there are only two or three days when a woman can fall pregnant. Therefore, the use of an ovulation kit is helpful.

Key Thought: If you keep your destination in focus, you will better manage navigation towards it.

Date:

Note / Prayers:

_____

_____

_____

_____

_____

_____

_____

_____

_____

_____

_____

_____

_____

_____

_____

_____

Testimonies Can Work a Miracle, Part 2

Remarkable testimonies abound of women who had no hope and, through prayer, got their desired miracle. The following are testimonies of a few women who faced challenges regarding their childbearing and the ensuing results.

I had been married for several years and had three miscarriages. I was beginning to believe that this was a punishment from God for not having sufficient faith in Him. A chance meeting with a church minister at a friend's house dispelled those thoughts, and through much prayer, deliverance and fasting, I conceived. I now have two children.

Lola, London, United Kingdom

I was told I would never be able to have children, and I had accepted it. I was very surprised when I became pregnant with no intervention. I now have a beautiful baby girl.

Anonymous

Monday: Ps. 50: 1–15

My Insight: The miracle you can turn into a testimony will come at exactly the right time – not a day early or late. Your victory is certain as long as you keep your side of the agreement. God is in total control of the situation, so don't panic.

Tuesday: Ps. 61

My Insight: Sometimes, circumstances that create testimonies do not come until our hearts are overwhelmed and we turn to God in deep, intensive prayer. Answered prayer is a heritage for those who fear God's name.

Wednesday: Ps. 57

My Insight: A heart fixed on God's faithfulness is necessary for victory.

Thursday: Ps. 70

My Insight: As you pray, deal with the spiritual forces that oppose conception. The psalmist did not ignore his opponents; he dealt with them in prayer. Sometimes, there may be a curse that has operated in a family for several generations.

Friday: Mark 10: 46–52

My Insight: When the Lord stood still, blind Bartimaeus's issue was resolved. May the Lord stand still as you cry out to Him with all your heart concerning your matter.

Saturday: Mark 9: 14–29

My Insight: True, living faith plus fasting and prayer are a powerful combination for a breakthrough in any area you face challenges.

Sunday: Luke 6: 6–10, 7: 1–10

My Insight: There is a supernatural power released to solve complex health problems when the Word of God is spoken over them.

Prayer Point:

Creative power of God, move in my womb by your fire, IJN.

Lord, let every obstacle on my path to supernatural conception and childbirth be cleared away by the blood of Jesus.

Take Note: There is a strong link between fertility and characteristics of modern lifestyles. Things such as convenience food, stressful work-life balance, smoking, drinking, and too much sugary food or drink can cause decreased sex drive and hormonal imbalances.

Key Thought: Continually remind yourself as you proceed on this journey, "I will laugh at last."

Date:

Note / Prayers:

_____

_____

_____

_____

_____

_____

_____

_____

_____

_____

_____

_____

_____

_____

_____

_____

_____

Week 6

God's Handwriting

It is a program written by God – a baby is born and knows when to draw in air even though he or she has survived via the mother's placenta in the womb. No one teaches this baby how to start breathing - it comes naturally. He or she keeps growing and knows when to roll over, sit, crawl, stand, walk, and run. This is incredible and awe-inspiring to watch. It's the same for pregnancy, a process specially manufactured by God to replenish mankind through the generations. It is a sacred program in God's laboratory – the masterpiece of His creation. If it brings heartbreak, sorrow, or pain, it is malfunctioning, and there is a reason why.

In many cases, the reasons for a miscarriage are unknown. The dark reality is that what cannot be explained in physical terms often has an invisible cause. To reveal the hidden destructive force, you need diagnostic prayers – prayers that act as a searchlight and can pierce through the clouds overshadowing your joy.

Monday: Ps. 113

My Insight: The Lord is the initiator of everything. He is the One who can make things happen and / or prevent them. He is the real deal, with the power to make things happen for you. Stay with Him, and you will be on the right track.

Tuesday: Ps. 48

My Insight: God is righteous and thus will always do what is right. He will turn your story into glory through His might and power.

Wednesday: Ps. 68: 3–35

My Insight: God has inherent and ultimate power, whereas every other authority on earth is received from Him.

Thursday: Ps. 89: 1–26

My Insight: Think back to the faithfulness of God that you have experienced in the past and reflect on it. If God was faithful then, He will be faithful now to fulfil your heart's desires.

Friday: Ps. 92

My Insight: Your horn will be exalted above your situation, and a time will come when you will rejoice and flourish in God's court.

Saturday: Ps. 94

My Insight: The Lord knows the battles we are facing and understands that we need help. He will rise up and fight for us in any situation we are being attacked.

Sunday: Ps 100 and 101

My Insight: God will fight for those who are faithful but not for the proud or deceitful. He puts a premium on our character when we walk with Him, especially when we are trust Him for a miracle.

Fact: One out of every ten pregnancies ends in miscarriage, and one in every four women will miscarry at some point in her reproductive years (UK) (4)

Prayer Point:

Lord, teach me to pray as I go on this journey.

Every harmful seed within me causing pregnancy to fail, be destroyed by the power of God, IJN.

Date:

Note / Prayers:

_____

_____

_____

_____

_____

_____

_____

_____

_____

_____

_____

_____

_____

_____

_____

_____

Week 7

Ask the Right Questions

I learnt this lesson the hard way in my quest for a child. Eighteen months after my husband and I got married, I had my first miscarriage. We were devastated and unaware of the battle ahead of us. I prayed and fasted and kept praying. Yet it was the beginning of a long and bitter battle, the dimensions of which I had no idea at the time. My journey of self-discovery took the better part of the next fifteen years. Following are the questions I asked, and you can use them to trigger your journey as well.

- Who am I?
- Why am I facing such a battle?
- What do I need to learn from this experience?
- How can I accelerate my advancement in this journey?
- Can I picture my final destination?

The answers will point you in the direction you need to go.

Monday: Ps. 69

My Insight: Sometimes, it's as though no one in the world is on your side. Remember – God always is.

Tuesday: Ps. 71

My Insight: God will deliver us from the hand of the wicked and show us where the battle is.

Wednesday: Ps. 74

My Insight: Does it feel as though God is not interested in your situation? PUSH (Pray Until Something Happens) to make Him unfold the mysteries of your specific battle and give you a testimony.

Thursday: Ps. 77

My Insight: To keep up your motivation, continually dwell on the goodness God showed you in the past.

Friday: Ps. 80

My Insight: Being childless may be a very lonely and painful journey. Many people may laugh at you in secret, while others share your pain but cannot speak. Only God can fight this battle for you, and He has insider knowledge. Hold on to Him.

Saturday: Ps. 86

My Insight: In the end, you are on your own with God. He is the only one who can make you triumph over shame.

Sunday: Ps. 88

My Insight: Sometimes, tears are the only way we can express desperation. I felt desperate a number of times, but after the tears, I was more determined to pray.

Prayer Point:

Lord, uncover my past, present, and future.

Reveal to me, Lord, what is hidden behind this problem, and help me to overcome in Jesus' name.

Fact: Your eggs are created when you are in the womb. A woman's supply of eggs, originally several million, is reduced by the time she reaches puberty.

The Egg (Oocyte)

The egg, also known as the oocyte, is the female gamete which passes on female DNA (chromosomal material) to offspring. It also controls the whole system necessary to bring male and female chromosomes together during the process of fertilization. Eggs are housed within a female's ovaries. At birth, girls have approximately one to two million eggs in their ovaries. By the time they reach puberty, this number decreases to about 300,000. At this time, the menstrual cycle or "period" begins which allows one egg to be released approximately every 28 days through a process known as ovulation. Over a woman's lifetime, only about 500 eggs are released from the ovaries. The remaining eggs gradually die out in the ovary when a woman goes through menopause. During the times when a woman is pregnant or takes birth control pills, eggs are not released from the ovaries.

www.med.nyu.edu/sti/content

Date:

Note / Prayers:

_____

_____

_____

_____

_____

_____

_____

_____

_____

_____

_____

_____

_____

_____

Healing after a Miscarriage

I was devastated after my first miscarriage. I couldn't believe that it had happened to me. But as I prayed, God healed me. It was the happy alternative to Humpty-Dumpty's experience – one minute I was shattered in pieces; the next, I was whole again. God put my heart back together again, and I felt as though it had never been broken to bits. Only God can give this supernatural healing. Ask Him sincerely, and He will act. You cannot afford to grieve for too long – you need to start trying again soon.

Monday: Ps. 56

My Insight: Our tears are precious to God. He keeps them in a bottle, writes about them in His book, and does not forget about them.

Tuesday: Ps. 57

My Insight: Some people's words are like sharp swords, but the Lord's mercy and grace is sufficient for all situations.

Wednesday: Ps. 60

My Insight: If we can establish a link to the throne room of God concerning our particular situation, God will arise.

Thursday: Ps. 61

My Insight: There will be times of trial when things are overwhelming – that's when the Lord is most present. Your strength shall be in quietness and confidence.

Friday: Ps. 62

My Insight: You must eliminate other options and stick to God to show you how to resolve the problem. Ultimate power belongs to Him.

Saturday: Ps. 63

My Insight: Even though your journey is a quest for a child, it is also a time for growing in faith and worship. Try not to let the anxiety of badly wanting a child overshadow your experience of worship.

Sunday: Pss. 64 and 65

My Insight: God has a sterling track record for answering prayers. Your situation will not be one where He fails.

Prayer Point:

Holy Spirit, make my womb super conducive for pregnancy, in Jesus' name.

Holy Spirit, by the same power that prepared the wombs of Elizabeth and Sarah, bind my egg and the sperm of my husband together to cause conception, in the name of Jesus.

Fact: Some physical symptoms can indicate your most fertile days: a rise in body temperature, mild abdominal pain, bloating, breast tenderness, increased sex drive, and changes in cervical mucus.

Date:

Note / Prayers:

_____

_____

_____

_____

_____

_____

_____

_____

_____

_____

_____

_____

_____

_____

_____

_____

Tailor-Made Solutions

In the quest for success in giving birth, there is no one-size-fits-all prescription or recommendation. Just as people are diverse in colour, race, and creed, we all have different circumstances. What works for another couple may not work for you and your husband, and what works for you may not work for them. Therefore, from the outset, focus on what you want. You may be quite happy to adopt to give an otherwise underprivileged child a chance for success as well as for the joy of bringing him or her up as your own, You may want to try the in vitro fertilization (IVF) technique as many times as your emotional and financial state allow, whilst another couple is dead set against the idea, preferring to wait to conceive naturally. Because the spectrum of possibilities on this journey is very wide, there is no right or wrong as long as the methods are above board. In other words, you have the right to choose how you will solve the issue of childlessness, and no one has the right to condemn you for the method you decide upon.

Monday: Ps. 16

My Insight: Your inheritance is colourful and bright. Leave nothing undone in the pursuit of claiming it.

Tuesday: Ps. 17

My Insight: Prayer is a heart-to-heart talk with God. He answers when it is deep and touching.

Wednesday: Ps. 18: 1–24

My Insight: God can be provoked to anger on your behalf.

Thursday: Ps. 18: 25–50

My Insight: He will train His own to fight and win the battle for the inheritance.

Friday: Ps. 20

My Insight: This psalm is a heartfelt prayer for victory in all of our endeavours and especially in this journey into fruitfulness. Pray and confess it often.

Saturday: Ps. 22

My Insight: This was a cry from the depth of Jesus' heart whilst going through His crucifixion, the words came from David's pen. You can adopt this psalm to express your depth of despair and enlist God's compassion, assistance, and victory.

Sunday: Ps. 29

My Insight: The voice of the Lord is suitable for all situations, and it brings His peace in the midst of a storm.

Prayer Point:

O Lord, the warrior, save me from the hands of wicked midwives, in the name of Jesus.

I render every weapon fashioned against my pregnancy impotent, in the name of Jesus.

O Lord, throw every Egyptian working against me into the midst of the sea, in the name of Jesus.

Fact: Your menstrual cycle is controlled by your pituitary gland, which is situated in your brain. It secretes hormones that travel through your bloodstream to regulate urine, temperature, growth, thyroid activity, and the production of fertility hormones in both men and women.

Date:

Note / Prayers:

_____

_____

_____

_____

_____

_____

_____

_____

_____

_____

_____

_____

_____

_____

_____

_____

_____

_____

Your Choice: Be Informed

You may be quite content to live with your childlessness, working for the good of children through missionary or charity work. However, acceptance should not be the result of giving up hope for bearing your own offspring. All things are possible with God.

You should not feel bad because you do not believe in IVF techniques despite their success in helping millions of couples achieve an otherwise impossible dream. At the same time, the couple who chooses to adopt another family's child as their own has the right to enjoy him or her in the same way as a biological parent. They have exercised their right of free choice. You should, however, choose carefully who you allow to counsel you medically and spiritually and reject any advice that is against God's ways.

Monday: Ps. 24

My Insight: It is comforting that the one who fights for you is the Lord of hosts – the king of glory Himself.

Tuesday: Ps. 25

My Insight: Meekness, a fruit of the Holy Spirit, is required to enlist God's help to fight our battles.

Wednesday: Ps. 26

My Insight: Again, it is worthy of note that God requires integrity of heart and lifestyle from us.

Thursday: Ps. 27

My Insight: If we wait on the Lord in faith, we will receive the strength to persevere until we reach ultimate victory.

Friday: Ps. 28

My Insight: When we seek God's face, let us remember to beseech Him to answer us favourably.

Saturday: Ps. 30

My Insight: A sojourn with the Lord as the leader ends in rejoicing.

Sunday: Ps. 31

My Insight: The Lord rewards those who diligently seek Him with victory.

Prayer Point:

I bind every spirit of mistake or failure assigned against my pregnancy, in the name of Jesus.

O Lord, send Your light before me to drive miscarriages from my womb and my life, IJN.

Info: In the old days, if a woman wasn't getting pregnant, people assumed that something was upsetting her – for example, she was having problems with her husband or her in-laws. Prevailing wisdom was that any kind of emotional disturbance could stop a woman from conceiving, and their instincts appeared to prove them right!

Date:

Note / Prayers:

_____

_____

_____

_____

_____

_____

_____

_____

_____

_____

_____

_____

_____

_____

_____

_____

_____

_____

 *Week 11*

Madam, There Is Nothing Medically Wrong with You

You should take any counsel you receive back to the Lord in prayer, to discern which advice to follow. Medically, I had several phases of counselling, as the teams of doctors we consulted at different stages each had techniques they wanted to try. At one point, I was advised to take two sets of injections daily – HCG (human chorionic gonadotropin) and an additional injection, which were both to keep my hormonal levels high enough to sustain the pregnancy. I did this diligently for three weeks and had not finished the course when I had yet another miscarriage. After one of the foremost authorities on fertility in Europe examined me, he found no defect and advised IVF to break the waiting period. I had not fallen pregnant for about two years, and time was ticking – I was forty years of age. Each piece of counsel was weighed and followed, but none yielded success. When the Creator stepped in, there was no contest. I became pregnant when I least expected it while my husband and I were still considering IVF. My baby was conceived and born naturally. The Lord saw me through the challenges and took all the glory.

Monday: Ps. 32

My Insight: You can be protected by God if there is no guile in your spirit.

Tuesday: Ps. 34

My Insight: Trust is a key ingredient in our relationship with God.

Wednesday: Ps. 35

My Insight: There are some battles that are too strong for us – we need the Lord to fight them on our behalf.

Thursday: Ps. 37: 1–20

My Insight: What are the desires of your heart? They shall be granted by the Lord.

Friday: Ps. 37: 21–40

My Insight: God guides the steps of a good person. Do you qualify?

Saturday: Ps. 40

My Insight: No matter how horrible the starting point is, the ending point can be glorious with God's help.

Sunday: Ps. 41

My Insight: True friends can only be identified by God or by trials. One's closest friends can be a disappointment in a time of need. Ask the Lord to lead you.

Prayer Point:

I bind the spirit of almost there. You will not operate in my life, in the name of Jesus.

I cast out every power attempting to prevent my children's conception.

Info: Infertility is much more prevalent today than in the days of our mothers. My mum could hardly recall any women who she knew who had problems conceiving.

Key Thought: Therefore I say to you, whatever things you ask when you pray, believe that you receive them, and you will have them. (Mk 11: 23–24). NKJV

Date:

Note / Prayers:

_____

_____

_____

_____

_____

_____

_____

_____

_____

_____

_____

_____

_____

_____

_____

Right Place, Right Time

To be perfectly honest, I had petitioned God to step in before I had to succumb to the IVF procedure recommended for me. My choice was to have my baby naturally. I have nothing against IVF, and I believe in its benefits, as mentioned earlier. However, God honoured my request. Against all medical odds, I conceived, and the Lord was with me during the pregnancy. I kept praying, and each step of the way, He held my hand and kept encouraging me daily.

Monday: Ps. 56

My Insight: During this journey, there will be fear and tears. At such times, God is near to calm our hearts and wipe our teardrops. This shows His tenderness towards us.

Tuesday: Ps. 57

My Insight: I will sing praises about God to the nations. Don't keep quiet about His goodness.

Wednesday: Ps. 60

My Insight: The passage says, "Judah is My sceptre" (v. 7). This means, in my opinion, that God would use Judah as a ruling authority in the earth. It is significant to note that our Lord Jesus Christ came from the tribe of Judah. Every individual has a mandate from God – mine is to share my testimony to bless all nations. What's yours?

Thursday: Ps. 61

My Insight: Our relationship with God is a two-way affair. God does His bit, and we do ours. Simple, isn't it?

Friday: Ps. 62

My Insight: No better friend exists than God. You can pour out your heart to Him and get the help you need.

Saturday: Ps. 63

My Insight: Our enemies will be put to shame, because it is God who fights for us.

Sunday: Pss. 64 and 65

My Insight: God is industrious, fruitful, and abundant. This must be reflected in the lives of His children.

Prayer Point:

O creative power of God, move in my womb by Your fire, in the name of Jesus.

I withdraw my womb from every evil altar, in the name of Jesus.

Info: An eighty-seven-year old friend of mine told me that in the past, when a woman had delays in conceiving, the belief was that she was putting too much pressure on herself and felt nervous. She was advised to calm down and work less.

Date:

Note / Prayers:

_____

_____

_____

_____

_____

_____

_____

_____

_____

_____

_____

_____

_____

_____

_____

_____

_____

_____

Winner Concepts 1

Having covered many options available in summaries up to this point, I will proceed to address trusting the Lord for natural conception (for surrogacy and sperm donation, please seek medical and spiritual counselling). I conceived naturally against all the odds, and this approach can also be used as a basis for strengthening your faith to trust the Lord while using any other method to aid your conception.

Your seven-step journey: WINNER CONCEPTS

aWareness

INquiry

diagNosis

prayER – preparation and diagnostic

CONCEPTion

Strategic preservation

Your mindset at the start of this journey should be that of a winner. Failure is not an option. Please take time to fast and pray with your husband or a friend over this issue before you embark on the course. Doing so helped me see what the challenges were, a lot more clearly.

Monday: Pss. 121 and 123;

My Insight: He will preserve your soul so that you don't become discouraged on this journey. Remember, a servant who wants to please her mistress watches her every move. In the same way, we should watch for God's moves.

Tuesday: Pss. 125 and 126

My Insight: Trusting in God in difficult times strengthens you to become immovable. One day, you will achieve your desire and feel drunk with joy.

Wednesday: Pss. 127 and 128

My Insight: God is the architect of our lives. Unless He is with you, every effort will fail. You must follow God's ways in order to be truly prosperous and successful.

Thursday: Pss. 130 and 131

My Insight: Have you ever felt totally dependent on God's mercy and grace? I have, and it's a good place to be. He is the only Person who can always deliver what we need. As we grow older, we ought to grow wiser. Additionally, calmness and humility are virtues to aspire for and practice, especially during this time of waiting.

Friday: Pss. 132 and 133

My Insight: David touched the heart of the Creator of the Universe and earned an eternal inheritance. Wow! I also desire to touch His heart in everything I do. Ask God how you can do so as well, and He will reveal Himself to you. Unity is a propelling force in the universe, so it is important to be in agreement with your husband over this and other matters. Do all that you can to avoid disagreements and unpleasantness.

Saturday: Pss. 134 and 135

My Insight: Lift up your hands to bless the Lord constantly – it will encourage you when you feel low and keep your eyes on the goal. What did God see in you that made Him choose you? I look at pictures of myself regularly and appreciate the beauty God has put in me. I then thank Him for all my good qualities and come up with a big smile!

Sunday: Ps. 136

My Insight: God is a good person – there is no ugliness in Him. Isn't that refreshing – someone with no hang-ups, no baggage, no warped or twisted opinions, and no hidden agendas? How exhilarating that we have a relationship with Him!

Prayer Point:

Every seed of failed pregnancy within me, be destroyed by the power of God, in Jesus' name.

Every satanic transfer or exchange regarding my womb, be destroyed by the power of God, in Jesus' name.

Fact: These days, there are still many unexplained cases of infertility. Many women, diagnosed with all sorts of conditions, do not respond to medical treatment. Yet often they are not advised to look at what is going on in their minds; rather, they are recommended medical procedures, such as courses of IVF.

Date:

Note / Prayers:

_____

_____

_____

_____

_____

_____

_____

_____

_____

_____

_____

_____

_____

_____

_____

Winner Concepts 2

Awareness

In many cases, when conception doesn't happen in an expected period, we become aware that there is a problem. This amount of time differs from couple to couple, but medically, if you have been having regular intercourse for two years, then there is an issue. That's the first level of awareness.

Monday: 2 Sam. 5: 12, Dan. 10: 7–21

My Insight: Awareness of a spiritual challenge is the first step in the recovery process. Ask God to help you realise what you are faced with. He can show you things others may not see. In fact, don't expect everyone – or perhaps anyone – to understand what you see or to feel the way you do. Sometimes it may be overwhelming.

Tuesday: Matt 8: 1–17

My Insight: Having contact with Jesus brings results. Your ultimate goal is to believe this.

Wednesday: John 9: 1–7

My Insight: Repeating this principle will engrave it in our hearts: obedience is the key to breakthrough. He promised, "I will instruct you and teach you in the way you should go." Obey Him.

Thursday: John 5: 1–14

My Insight: Jesus can heal us, but sin can make any ailment return. Have you dealt with the presence of sin in your life? Is there any habit you have not repented of? If so, why not deal with it now?

Friday: Ps. 34

My Insight: God guarantees that He will always answer His children's requests. That answer, though, may be yes, no, or wait. Have you heard your answer yet?

Saturday: Judg. 13: 2–25

My Insight: While you are waiting and praying, you may have a divine encounter – prepare your mind. Anything can happen on this journey.

Sunday: Josh. 1: 1–9

My Insight: The Lord your God will be with you in all that you do as you obey Him. You will have your testimony by His grace.

Prayer Point:

I bind and cast out every spirit of failure from all procedures, in the name of Jesus.

Every word spoken by the enemy against my ability to conceive, be destroyed by the power of God, in the name of Jesus.

Fact: Anything we do to help ourselves conceive will not be effective if our minds are not peaceful.

Key Thought: The testing of your faith produces patience. Jam. 1: 3 NKJV

Date:

Note / Prayers:

_____

_____

_____

_____

_____

_____

_____

_____

_____

_____

_____

_____

_____

_____

_____

_____

_____

Week 15

Winner Concepts 3

Inquiry

After this, we move to the inquiry stage, where we ask questions. Most people would automatically ask medical questions and go for a series of tests. These may reveal certain defects which need medical intervention. Consequently, successful treatment can be administered. However, the spiritual aspect is still highly neglected. This deep area is a mystery to many and remains so till this day.

Due to the vast array of techniques available for medical intervention, I will not treat medical analysis in this devotional in any more depth. In the United Kingdom, the chance for miscarriage in a woman's first pregnancy, as I mentioned earlier, is one in four, or 25 per cent (in the United States, about 10 to 15 percent among women who know they are pregnant (www.marchofdimes.org) and in Nigeria, the available statistics are inconclusive). Of these statistics, the causes are recorded as unknown in a high number of the cases. That is, no one can explain medically why the miscarriages occur.

If you have experienced a miscarriage and the devastation it can cause, you will have felt the agony and pain that accompanies it. No matter how many children a woman has had, losing a baby has a most damaging effect on her mind. People are well-meaning in their attempts to comfort, offering such statements as, "Don't worry, you will have another child."

Unknown to them, internally, the grieving woman is screaming "No, no, no, you don't understand – it's this one I want, not another child." Nothing can take the place of a baby lost in miscarriage, because each one is individual and special. Each couple trying to conceive needs a beam of light to push back the confusion and bewilderment concealing the cause of the problem and disperse them.

Monday: Josh. 3: 1–17

My Insight: The priesthood is meant to make the waters of challenge part. Is your priesthood effective? Can God use you to show His glory to the world?

Tuesday: Gen. 25.20-26

My Insight:

The reason for Rebekah's eventful pregnancy was shrouded in mystery, until she enquired of the Lord who explained it to her. She was troubled He clarified the situation she as faced with.

Wednesday: Dan. 2: 5–24

My Insight: Analysis can take place through dreams as God reveals the invisible.

Thursday: Neh. 4: 1–23

My Insight: One hand on the business of life and one on the warfare front – that's the approach to have when faced with a challenge like this one.

Friday: Ruth 3: 1–18

My Insight: Someone guided Ruth on how to have a happy ending. I pray that this information will similarly act as a guide, and I trust the Lord that you will rejoice at last.

Saturday: Esther 8: 1–9: 3

My Insight: Esther and Mordecai turned the attack of Haman back towards him – he perished. Likewise, may the Lord turn back the battle onto any enemy responsible for the challenges you are facing.

Sunday: Eph. 6: 10–18

My Insight: There is no question that a war is going on in the spiritual realm over your matter. Enemy forces that cannot be seen require you to use weapons that are invisible, but God will help you every step of the way.

Prayer Point:

By the power that divided the Red Sea, I lay hold of my babies, in the name of Jesus.

Holy Spirit, make my womb super conducive for pregnancy, in the name of Jesus.

Fact: People who are stressed are subject to mood swings, anxiety, panic attacks, depression, and anger. The physical and chemical results act as a contraceptive, undetected and undiagnosed in many cases.

Date:

Note / Prayers:

_____

_____

_____

_____

_____

_____

_____

_____

_____

_____

_____

_____

_____

_____

_____

Winner Concepts 4

Diagnosis

Every problem-solving process starts with accurate diagnosis. If it is inaccurate, you risk wasting time, effort, and money chasing an invisible tail. This week, you must ask yourself some soul-searching questions. Just like a tree knows where its roots are hidden, you know your background and some of the circumstances under which you were born, brought up, married, and conceived. Any evil hidden causes which are likened to roots need to be exposed and uprooted so they cease blocking the path to your miracle. The following can be common categories. If you have any of these in your background, there is a need to pray intensively for the effects to be removed.

- A polygamous background – your mum was one of many wives or had children by different men or your dad had multiple partners or wives
- Your conception, if outside of wedlock
- Evil dedication – that is, to family gods or water spirits from conception or afterwards
- Worshippers of snakes or idols in your family line
- A loose sexual lifestyle
- Sexual intercourse outside marriage
- Exposure to witchcraft activities viewed as child's play
- Knowingly despising God in the past (e.g., Michal, daughter of Saul).

These are some common spiritual reasons which may account for delay in pregnancy or miscarriage and by no means a complete list. They are indicators to make you aware that the causes are present and can be tackled in prayer. When you can identify the problem, your battle is half won. The discovery may also lift the lid on other inroads the enemy may have made into your life.

Monday:

Tuesday: Isa. 40: 1–15

My Insight: God will assure you that he is leading you through this stage.

Wednesday: Isa. 38

My Insight: A cake of figs was the antidote for Hezekiah. What is the medicine for what you are facing now?

Thursday: Zech. 4: 1–9

My Insight: Your hands have laid the foundation of this journey, and they will finish it with God's help.

Friday: Isa. 25: 1–10

My Insight: He will destroy mourning and bring you a new song.

Saturday: Isa. 26: 1–13

My Insight: I always rejoice at the thought that I have a life Companion who is capable, dependable, and knowledgeable.

Sunday: Isa. 27

My Insight: When your future is predicted, you can go forward in the strength of the conviction that you will laugh last. Therefore, let fear be expelled from your heart as you go through this stage. If there are any changes to make, do so with a repentant heart.

Prayer Point:

I bind and arrest every infection that may wish to be present in my body, in the name of Jesus.

Blood of Jesus, nullify the effects of any drug administered to me, in the name of Jesus.

Fact: Many women do not know they are stressed. According to research, however, hidden stress can lead to disease and depression.

Date:

Note / Prayers:

_____

_____

_____

_____

_____

_____

_____

_____

_____

_____

_____

_____

_____

_____

_____

_____

Winner Concepts 5

Prayer – Assurance

Assurance undergirds the whole journey. This is a calming certainty that God is on your side and wants the same result for you as the one you desire. It will bring Him glory and you great joy. Rest assured in this knowledge during the rough times when all you can do is cry yourself to sleep from exhaustion, frustration, or both. Prepare your mind for the long haul, and if the journey is short, rejoice and enjoy it. If it's long, then you will be strong enough to bear the pressures of waiting. When you face a problem, you naturally run to the person who can help you. In my quest for a successful pregnancy, I ran to all who listened until I realised the futility of my many-sided approach. As with anything in life, you need to focus on a chosen path and follow it single-mindedly.

Monday: Ps. 126

My Insight: When the Lord turns your story around, it is like a dream. Keep this in mind as you go forward.

Tuesday: Ps. 30

My Insight: Picture yourself rejoicing. This will help you as you press forward.

Wednesday: Ps. 20

My Insight: God will answer His anointed people.

Thursday: Ps. 26.3;

My Insight: A good self-assessment is always important on this journey, as it will enable you to remain close to the Lord while you deal with any impediments.

Friday: Heb. 2: 1–18

My Insight: We have a faithful and compassionate High Priest committed to our success.

Saturday: Zech. 4: 1–10

My Insight: A ceaseless supply of oil is your portion.

Sunday: Zech. 4: 11–14

My Insight: You are the anointed of the Lord. Rejoice!

Prayer Point:

Holy Spirit, by the same power that prepared the womb of Elizabeth and Sarah, bind my egg and the sperm of my husband together to cause conception, in the name of Jesus.

I break every evil spiritual stone or goat destroying my children in pregnancy, in the name of Jesus.

Action: Ask yourself this question: why do I want a child? If you want it for a selfish reason, this could be a reason why a baby hasn't come yet.

Date:

Note / Prayers:

_____

_____

_____

_____

_____

_____

_____

_____

_____

_____

_____

_____

_____

_____

_____

_____

_____

Week 18

Winner Concepts 6

Prayer – Diagnostic

Due to the mysterious nature of the spiritual aspect of childlessness, diagnostic prayers need to be said to expose the roots of the problem. These prayers should be aggressive in the sense that you will generate some body heat as you pray with intensity. The Bible records the prayer styles of Jesus and Elijah – two people who achieved many results in prayer. When He prayed on the Mount of Olives, Jesus released bodily fluids because of the intense pressure He experienced. Similarly, if during the course of your prayers, you find yourself sweating in an air-conditioned room, you are on the right track. As the saying goes, the end justifies the means. For such a deeply spiritual exercise, you need to determine that you will exercise whatever spiritual strength you can muster and apply yourself to the prayers, as this will open up previously unknown depths in your life. This is the next level towards becoming aware of the presence of unseen causes.

Monday: Esth 4.16,17

My Insight: Your resolve should make you go to any lengths to obtain your blessing.

Tuesday: Heb 5.7

My Insight: Jesus paid a high price for his victory, emulate Him.

Wednesday: Ps. 20

My Insight: God will answer His anointed people.

Thursday: James 5.17,18

My Insight: Elijah had his weaknesses but God heard his cries.

Friday: Judg 4.14

My Insight: Deborah arose in a time of turmoil and her courage saved a nation.

Saturday: Acts 12.5-17

My Insight: The prayers of the disciples were instrumental in the release of Peter from prison. Prayers generate freedom.
Sunday: Rev 8.3,4

My Insight: Your prayers are reaching God's throne, don't stop!

Prayer Point:

Any object that the enemy is using to destroy or delay my pregnancy, remove it, in the name of Jesus.

O Lord, let Your strong east wind blow against the Red Sea in my womb now, in the name of Jesus.

Info: One of the most common barriers to conception is the feeling of hopelessness caused by deep desperation. In many instances, as soon as you stop being desperate for something, that thing becomes available. Many women confirm that this is true in their quest to get pregnant.

Date:

Note / Prayers:

_____

_____

_____

_____

_____

_____

_____

_____

_____

_____

_____

_____

_____

_____

_____

Winner Concepts 7

Strategic Preservation

Abstinence from habits that do not add value to your life and purpose.

The choice to abstain may mean losing some friends who cannot see where you are going. The journey through childlessness can be a lonely road, and there may be people who should not be travelling with you – like Lot was not meant to stay with Abraham. The choice to take Lot along contradicted God's original instruction to Abraham and I suspect, may have delayed God's program for Abraham's life. Other vices will be impediments in this quest for success in the same way that abuse of drugs affects an athlete's performance. Examples of these include too much sleep, idleness, gossiping, overindulgence in TV, anger, malice, bitterness, and so forth.

In contrast, abstinence from these activities gives you the strength to persevere in the face of temporary disappointment. You will need to build up your resistance to be like armour, so that you are immune to the enemy's arrows of discouragement and tongues of judgement and cruelty.

Absolute Focus

You need to be absolutely focused to achieve your desired result. This means not allowing anything or anyone, no matter how close they are, to distract you from your goal. You will need time and energy to carry out your prayers. And when the going gets tough, praying will help fill the dry patches with strength you did not know you possessed.

Monday: Isa. 50. 7

My Insight: Absolute focus is crucial in seeking God's face for a miracle.

Tuesday: Luke 17: 3–4

My Insight: Forgive those around you easily. Don't be a difficult person.

Wednesday: Neh. 2: 10–16

My Insight: Sometimes, as you focus intently, no one needs to hear what you are doing, not even your close friends. This aids your concentration for proper planning.

Thursday: Colossians 3: 1–17

My Insight: Work on revamping your entire character, starting this week.

Friday: Gal. 5: 13–26

My Insight: Reinforce your love for those around you by your words and actions.

Saturday: Eph. 4: 29–32

Keep a close watch on the words that you speak.

Sunday: Col. 2: 13–14

Check your heart to ensure that you have forgiven yourself for any mistakes or wrong decisions you may have made from the past, that you blame yourself for.

Prayer Point:

Every demonic instrument operating to abort my pregnancy, be broken to pieces, in the name of Jesus.

O Lord, fight against the destroyer working against my increase and fruitfulness, in the name of Jesus.

Info: If you are a happy, clear-minded person with no inner blocks, obsessive behaviours, or desperation, it is likely that you will conceive quicker.

Date:

Note / Prayers:

_____

_____

_____

_____

_____

_____

_____

_____

_____

_____

_____

_____

_____

_____

_____

_____

_____

_____

Week 20

Travelling Light

You need to exercise patience and have an open mind. Also, brace yourself for shocking discoveries. Many things and people you took for granted will appear in a different light once the beams of revelation expose them. Cast unforgiveness aside, as it will impede your progress and colour your outlook. You cannot afford to be weighed down with baggage. Travelling light will enable you to reach your destination.

Monday: Matt. 5: 1–12

My Insight: Developing the right attitude should be an ongoing project throughout life. If you haven't started it before, now is the perfect time.

Tuesday: Matt. 7: 1–14

My Insight: A positive attitude includes a realistic evaluation of self. Ask God to reveal anything inside you that may be a hindrance to your prayers. I did, and He was kind enough to show them to me and help me work on myself.

Wednesday: Mic. 7: 6–9

My Insight: You are in for some surprises – any journey of spiritual warfare uncovers enemies. Strengthen your heart therefore to face some hurtful truths.

Thursday: John 5: 7–18

My Insight: There are those who will not be happy when your story changes – don't worry about them. Rejoice and celebrate the goodness of the Lord in the land of the living.

Friday: 1 Thess. 5: 14–15, Jude 20, 1 Cor. 15: 58

My Insight: Be a good example to all, and encourage others to overcome their weaknesses as you also work on yours. Keep serving diligently.

Saturday: Ps. 35

My Insight: God will fight this battle on your behalf, and the enemies who planned to treat you with scorn will be forced to back down.

Sunday: Eph. 4: 17–5: 1

My Insight: Our lives should reflect God's presence. He is faithful and will reward your labour of love.

Prayer Point:

Any curse strengthened by the enemy of my pregnancy, be broken by the blood of Jesus.

Every strongman supervising my womb to arrest the creation of babies, be destroyed in the name of Jesus.

Fact: When it comes to conception, stress is the condition that's the most dangerous and most talked about.

Date:

Note / Prayers:

_____

_____

_____

_____

_____

_____

_____

_____

_____

_____

_____

_____

_____

_____

_____

_____

Week 21

Praise under Pressure

One would think that the people who know of your situation will be sympathetic and careful to manage what they say around you but that is not always the case. You must develop a mechanism to deal with this cruelty.

Firstly, don't allow yourself to dwell on what they say. Let their words pass over you like water off a duck's back. How you react is a matter of choice – positively or negatively – and you can choose to be happy or unhappy. Occupy yourself with worthwhile projects to take your mind off the issues whilst actively praying and following your medical program so that you release yourself from the stress of lengthy vigils, inevitable test results, and so on. For example, I took the opportunity to learn new songs, write them down, and sing them. I also decided to spend time worshipping the Lord, so I dedicated whole days to doing this. That, for me, was a sacrifice of praise, and it yielded outstanding results – grace that was humanly impossible.

Monday: 1 Sam. 17: 20–29

My Insight: Those who should have been happy that David had a solution were actually jealous and nasty. This did not stop God from carrying out His plan.

Tuesday: Ps. 45: 1–20

My Insight: As long as you maintain a righteous lifestyle in this morally corrupt world, the Lord will lift you up, and you will have joy.

Wednesday: Jer. 1: 1–12

My Insight: It was God who called you, and He will keep you from fearing insults and other harmful comments.

Thursday: Ps. 150

My Insight: Let praise be the fabric of your world, and the Lord will stay close to you during this journey and beyond.

Friday: Isa. 1: 1–10

My Insight: When you approach God for His help, you must be innocent of accusing others. Examine yourself to see if you have accused anyone, and if you have, repent.

Saturday: Ps. 42: 1–11

My Insight: There are bound to be moments when the taunts make you feel less than your best. At such times, put your hope in God again, as you will soon have a testimony of His faithfulness.

Sunday: Ps. 149: 1–9

My Insight: Humility is a prerequisite for victory when God is fighting your battles.

Prayer Point

Blood of Jesus, cleanse me and show me mercy, in the name of Jesus.

Every evil controlling force being used to manipulate my pregnancy, be consumed by fire, in Jesus' name.

Fact: Unhappiness, hopelessness, anxiety, despair, agony, torture, misery, defiance, and heartache can all arise out of desperation and are harmful to the body.

Date:

Note / Prayers:

_____

_____

_____

_____

_____

_____

_____

_____

_____

_____

_____

_____

_____

_____

_____

_____

The Power of Words

Secondly, use the Word of God as your shield by memorising certain scriptures to counter their words. Remember, "Death and life are in the power of the tongue: and they that love it shall eat the fruit thereof" (Prov. 18: 21). Don't allow any negative words to find a resting place in your life. Instead, counter their negative comments with a positive confession from God's word in a non-confrontational way. In other words, if someone tells you that it is best to have your last baby by the time you are thirty-eight years of age, let them know that there is nothing too hard for the God of all people – He is able to do all things. Testimonies abound, both in the Bible and in present day, of women who God has helped conceive despite their challenges. Nothing is beyond God's knowledge, wisdom, and expertise; the depths of His resources are staggering. Every discovery in medical science is a result of God's knowledge being shared with humankind, and the benefits are for the good of man. He wants us to have the knowledge to meet the diverse needs in the area of childlessness and childbirth.

Monday: Heb. 4: 12–16

My Insight: The word of God has no equal – it destroys everything that needs to be destroyed and builds up everything that needs to be built up. Use it to your advantage.

Tuesday: 2 Cor. 10: 1–6

My Insight: Words are invisible arrows which can manifest in discouragement, lack of faith, spiritual stagnancy, and depression.

Wednesday: Rev. 12: 9–17

My Insight: The war you are fighting is part of the wrath the enemy shows against God's children. Rejoice and be glad, for the Lord is fighting for you, and the elements can work in your favour (e.g., the land swallowing up the water from the dragon's mouth).

Thursday: Phil. 4: 8–9

My Insight: Thinking of things that will build you up rather than pulling you down brings God's peace.

Friday: Jer. 29: 10–14

My Insight: Take God's promise to be found by the diligent soul as your inspiration to seek him until it is fulfilled.

Saturday: Jer. 23: 21–29

My Insight: The true word of God has an impact. The counterfeit does not.

Sunday: Matt. 12: 30–37

My Insight: Let your heart be in a state of peace so that you can confidently speak words of peace and faith even when you are provoked. Otherwise, you will react with fear.

Prayer Point:

O man of war, save me out of the hands of wicked midwives, in the name of Jesus.

I render every weapon fashioned against my pregnancy impotent, in the name of Jesus.

Info: Negative emotions have the same effect on someone's body as removing the screws from a computer, one by one. Eventually, it will fall apart.

Date:

Note / Prayers:

_____

_____

_____

_____

_____

_____

_____

_____

_____

_____

_____

_____

_____

_____

_____

_____

Week 23

Angel

The arrival of your angel, as I like to put it, is an unprecedented event. Nothing can prepare you for the joy that a baby brings after a period of waiting. The laughter, celebrations, and euphoria are of heavenly proportions. It is truly worth the blood, sweat, and tears. All pain, sorrow, and despair vanish in the face of such unspeakable joy. Just as tears of disappointment flowed, now there are tears of joy. Take time to visualise your son or daughter and let your face light up with a smile.

Monday: Ps. 126: 1–6

My Insight: No matter how many times I read this psalm, it still has the power to lift me to untold heights of joy.

Tuesday: Luke 2: 8–20

My Insight: An angel announced Jesus' birth. And God's word says none shall be barren in His household, so this promise shall surely come to pass in your life, in Jesus' name.

Wednesday: Isa. 9: 1–10

My Insight: The land of gloom became a land of light and joy. Every person's life is a land – what is yours made of?

Thursday: Ps. 147: 1–13

My Insight: God is impressed by those who fear Him.

Friday: Ps. 128: 1–6

My Insight: The blessings of God upon the house of those who fear Him are abundant.

Saturday: 1 Tim. 1: 12–17

My Insight: Strange as it may seem, the more severe a problem is, the greater the joy when it is resolved. Your testimony will glorify God in the end.

Sunday: 1 Pet. 1: 1–16

My Insight: Experiences of those who have gone before serve as encouragement for us as we contend with similar challenges. Their stories inspire us.

Prayer Point:

O Lord, throw every Egyptian working against me into the midst of the sea, in the name of Jesus.

I shut down every satanic network fashioned against my pregnancy, in the name of Jesus.

Info: There is a difference between being desperate for a baby and believing that a baby you deeply desire will be yours. You need to get off the desperation wagon and transfer to the wagon of faith!

Date:

Note / Prayers:

_____

_____

_____

_____

_____

_____

_____

_____

_____

_____

_____

_____

_____

_____

_____

_____

_____

Week 24

Remarkable

God wrote the program for the fallopian tubes and ovaries to cooperate to produce the egg. The man's reproductive organs produce the sperm, and they move their way quickly through the tubes, and against all odds, break through to pierce and fertilise an egg (or two or more), and the fertilised egg moves into the uterus to implant in the wall and grow over nine months to become a baby. Quite remarkable, isn't it?

If this doesn't happen, it's an indication that the program has gone wrong, and there is a process to identify the root cause of the malfunction. As we all know, some medical consultants have a better understanding of gynaecological problems than others. The same applies spiritually – some have a natural skill for treating women facing the challenge of childlessness, others haven't. The best consultants have a high degree of empathy - to feel what you feel and to be where you are. Sometimes, part of the divine plan is to help us feel the pain of delay so that when it is over, we can encourage others with the added benefit of experience.

Monday: Luke1: 1–4

My Insight: Something went wrong for Elizabeth. On this occasion, it was God's doing. Have you taken time to find out if it may be the same in your situation? In the end, she rejoiced, just as you also will.

Tuesday: 1 Sam. 1: 1–8

My Insight: Hannah allowed her situation to continue for several years. When she decided to do something about it, her breakthrough came. Where are you in this journey? Have you reached the point where you say "enough is enough"?

Wednesday: Luke 1: 36–40

My Insight: It was an angel who informed Mary of Elizabeth's state, not a human being – possibly because no human being apart from Zechariah knew. Mary responded instantly and, moved by revelation, went to visit Elizabeth. Are you moving by revelation from heaven? God still communicates today, and angels are still sent to earth on assignment.

Thursday: 1 Cor. 1: 1–11

My Insight: Do you have contentions with anyone in your life? Scan your heart and relationships to ensure they are not causing divisions. A peaceful countenance, life, and heart are necessary for anything in our lives to be made right by heaven.

Friday: Matt. 13: 24–30

My Insight: Any malfunction is evidence that something has gone wrong in a system. Finding out what this is may mean some discomfort while the transformation takes place and the solution is reached.

Saturday: Prov. 31: 25–31

My Insight: She is clothed with strength and honour so that she can pray for a desired conclusion. She will be called a mother in time to come and praised by her husband and her household.

Sunday: Prov. 15: 1–15

My Insight: We can cultivate the key virtue of using our tongues effectively. Waiting on God should affect every aspect of our lives, especially our choice of words.

Prayer Point:

I will see the great work of the Lord as I deliver my children safely, in the name of Jesus.

I refuse to harbour any pregnancy killer in any area of my life, in the name of Jesus.

Info: Not all happy people have an easy life. But they know how to have faith. As a result, their trials have better outcomes daily. Positive attitudes have the power to affect one's life outcomes for the better.

Date:

Note / Prayers:

_____

_____

_____

_____

_____

_____

_____

_____

_____

_____

_____

_____

_____

_____

_____

_____

_____

Week 25

Trump, the Teacher

At one stage, I switched the channel whenever he came on or ignored any book or article he was featured in. I only saw the brash, larger-than-life personality that went with his name and the lavish lifestyle that I thought was over the top. I wasn't impressed by such a loudmouth, and nothing he did was of any interest to me – until I watched *The Apprentice*. After the first episode I saw, I was hooked. I became a Donald Trump supporter if not fan. I considered what he said and realised that he seemed quite sincere. Maybe at his age, he has nothing to lose, so he tells the truth in the best way he knows possible. His experiences have formed a body of knowledge for him to help those coming up the ladder, and he is generous with it.

Monday: Acts 9: 1–12

My Insight: Saul had an encounter which opened his eyes and made him a teacher of many. Similarly, encountering trials helps you teach those going through a similar experience.

Tuesday: Eph. 4: 21–25

My Insight: We should tell each other the truths that no one else will, but it must be done in the spirit of love.

Wednesday: 1 Pet. 2: 20–24

My Insight: Be an example to others of how your trials demonstrate following in Jesus footsteps.

Thursday: 1 Cor. 9: 19–22

My Insight: Your calling is to help others, and this is the training ground.

Friday: 2 Cor. 4: 15–18

My Insight: All will end in the glory of God.

Saturday: 1 Cor. 9: 23–27

My Insight: A disciplined approach to our lives is required before, during, and after trials. This will help us remain down-to-earth in the midst of both adversity and plenty.

Sunday: Rom. 8: 28

My Insight: Every step of a Christian's journey is planned strategically by God. He can use even the most difficult incidents as a stepping stone to a good thing.

Prayer Point

Every horse and rider in my womb, family, or office, be thrown into the sea, in the name of Jesus.

I bind every spirit of error assigned against my pregnancy, in the name of Jesus.

Fact: A woman who discovered that her husband could not have children decided to adopt a baby girl after nine years of trying. Three months later, she got pregnant! How? She stopped trying so hard.

Date:

Note / Prayers:

_____

_____

_____

_____

_____

_____

_____

_____

_____

_____

_____

_____

_____

_____

_____

_____

_____

_____

God Shows Up

To receive a miracle from God, you need to assess your mindset. Our current technological advancements have conditioned us towards impatience. If one method fails, we try another without perseverance. Our approach to prayer is much the same. Realistically, how long is too long? That is a question each couple has to answer for themselves – many feel a year or two is too long, whilst some wait for twenty years before they pursue other methods. Sarah was ninety, and Elizabeth had entered menopause, yet God still showed up for them. Likewise, God will show up for you at the appointed time, but you should not remain static. You should pursue the solution diligently in the spiritual and medical arenas to get your desired result.

Monday: Isa. 50: 7

My Insight: Our laser-focused determination demands an answer from heaven.

Tuesday: 2 Tim. 1: 12

My Insight: When you are depending on someone for a miracle, that person's character is important. The Lord is trustworthy, and the outcome will be positive.

Wednesday: Matt. 7: 7 – verse for the next three days.

My Insight: If we ask correctly, it shall be given. We need to invest time, effort, and energy to ensure that we are not asking amiss.

Thursday: Matt. 7: 7

My Insight: In addition to asking, you must research solutions that are acceptable to the Most High.

Friday: Matt. 7: 7

My Insight: Persistent knocking, in the literal sense, represents a nuisance and demands a response. We need to have a continuous approach to prayer and other efforts to receive an answer.

Saturday: Luke 18: 8

My Insight: Keep praying until the Lord makes a way that the answer will come and that there is no doubt. Will He find faithfulness in you, or will you have given up?

Sunday: Luke 11: 13

My Insight: This reading gives a good picture of God's willingness to bless His children. He is our most passionate supporter and fan. Think about that!

Prayer Point:

O Lord, send Your light before me to drive miscarriages away from my womb and my life, in the name of Jesus.

I bind the spirit of almost there. You will not operate in my life, in the name of Jesus.

Reflect: Are you focusing on the beauty of life or the ugliness? Is your mind free or worried – accepting or prejudiced?

Date:

Note / Prayers:

_____

_____

_____

_____

_____

_____

_____

_____

_____

_____

_____

_____

_____

_____

_____

_____

_____

_____

_____

Rest

Sometimes, all it takes for modern women to successfully conceive is rest. Sophia Loren's story echoes that of a woman who lived several generations ago – Elizabeth, the mother of John the Baptist. She was the wife of a priest, a woman of God in her own right, and yet she had lived with reproach all her life. In the Jewish tradition as in the African tradition, the inability to produce offspring is looked down on. The women carry a stigma in society. Some marriages break up as a result of this condition; sometimes, the in-laws would instigate divorce proceedings. When Elizabeth became pregnant, she couldn't handle the prying eyes, the wagging tongues, or the speculation of the evil observers. So she hid for five months until her pregnancy was established and impossible to deny. Do you too need rest from the hustle and bustle of life or from prying eyes?

Monday: Matt. 11: 28

My Insight: Rest is not only physical but also mental. A peaceful setting is necessary to care for a pregnancy.

Tuesday: 1 Sam. 1: 5, 8

My Insight The support of a partner is crucial in this resting period.

Wednesday: 1 Sam. 1: 4–7

My Insight: The evil observers are still around during this time, but ask for the grace to remain quiet and to prevent them from getting under your skin. Avoid contact with them at all costs.

Thursday: 1 Sam. 2: 1–5

My Insight: When God fights your battles, those who once scorned you become your friends and are compelled to rejoice with you.

Friday: Isa. 30: 18–21

My Insight: God, defender of the weak, is your greatest ally.

Saturday: Heb. 10: 35–39

My Insight: Persevere in your place of rest.

Sunday: Heb. 6: 12–20

My Insight: Patience leads to inheriting promises.

Prayer Point:

I cast out every power blocking my children, in the name of Jesus.

I break every grip of witchcraft over my pregnancy, in the name of Jesus.

Reflect: Do you live in the present and enjoy it, or are you distracted by the past or future? Do you love life and see innocence, or hate your life and see mostly evil?

Date:

Note / Prayers:

_____

_____

_____

_____

_____

_____

_____

_____

_____

_____

_____

_____

_____

_____

_____

_____

_____

Taking Time Off

You must take whatever steps necessary to preserve your physical and emotional condition during this time. Have you been waiting for a long period of time? Are you stressed or in a high-powered job where you are always on the go? In her five months of seclusion, Elizabeth must have checked her appearance in a mirror several times a day if she possessed one. She would have been in a state of shock and disbelief mixed with deep joy that comes from knowing her miracle was true. She gained confidence that this was an answered prayer, not just a dream. She was over the moon.

Do you think you need to hide away and pray? Will it do you good to stay away from friends and foes? Why don't you consider taking some time off, away from their prying eyes? Some people can discern pregnancy from day one. Therefore, you may need to hide away as Elizabeth did to increase the Lord's spiritual covering over you. Your season may be longer than five months. If the Lord tells you to hide as He did me, many may be offended, and you may not understand why. However, if this happens when you are following the Lord's instruction, then His direction takes precedence over human emotions. Pray and allow the Lord to guide you. True friends will understand when all becomes clear.

Monday: Ps. 116: 1–14, 18

My Insight: The sentence, "I will pay my vows", comes up twice in the same psalm to point out that it is essential. As a worshipper waiting on the Lord for the gift of a new life, make a vow – an offering to the Lord – that costs you. In other words, it should not just be convenient or done in exchange for something from God.

Tuesday: Isa. 28: 5–13

My Insight: We must follow a process to make things come to pass. In this situation, it is important to remove or avoid all negative factors – stress in your mind or body, bad diet, unsatisfying relationships, and bad lifestyle habits like smoking, drinking, drugs, and so forth.

Wednesday: Jer. 30: 10, 17–22

My Insight: Everyone waiting on the Lord for a child will at times need a word of encouragement or a gentle "fear not". The secret is to obey and indeed not be afraid.

Thursday: Matt. 11: 28–30, Jer. 27: 22

My Insight: The yoke Christ expects His children to carry is not heavy and it varies from one person to another.

Friday: Ps. 23

My Insight: Everyone needs a shepherd that knows where he or she is taking you. Following the shepherd ensures you do not get lost and wander around in the wilderness.

Saturday: 2 Cor. 10: 1–8

My Insight: This journey is a battle in which physical weapons are not the modus operandi – only spiritual weapons will win this war.

Sunday: 1 Cor. 13: 7–13

My Insight: This battle needs to be conducted in an atmosphere of love. That may sound like a paradox, but the ideal condition for success is an environment with no conflict. Sometimes, the situation is turbulent, but you must strive to keep calm amidst the circumstances to achieve your goal. This will require much prayer and self-control.

Ps. 14: 3–7

My Insight: This reading provides deep insight into what could be going on in the spiritual realm around a lack of conception. There are high rates of unexplained infertility, and the cause may be spiritual, not physical.

Prayer Point:

From today onwards, I shall not cast aside my young, in the name of Jesus.

I paralyse every opposition to my pregnancy, in the name of Jesus.

I receive deliverance from the spirit of monthly anxiety and nervousness, in the name of Jesus.

Reflect: Do you focus on doing what you can and learning from your mistakes, or do you focus on reliving your mistakes, constantly chastising yourself and others?

Date:

Note / Prayers:

_____

_____

_____

_____

_____

_____

_____

_____

_____

_____

_____

_____

_____

_____

_____

_____

Peace

When she emerged after her period of hiding, Elizabeth's posture must have changed. No longer did she seethe in silent pain when she walked down the street, being greeted by young teenage girls, who were married with babies. And she was no longer a topic of discussion in her town regarding how God had forsaken Zachariah and her in that area. She didn't cry herself to sleep at night or feel knots in her stomach whenever she heard the announcement that another young wife was expecting.

How you carry yourself before and after you conceive, no matter how long you have waited, matters to the Most High. You need to maintain peace in your heart so that stress, anxiety, and worry do not rob you of your joy. Your condition has a solution, but if you allow fear into your heart, it drives out the faith which you need to receive a miracle from God. Faith keeps a smile on your face, a song in your heart, and a rock-solid belief that your sun will surely shine in His time.

Monday: Heb. 10: 23–30

My Insight: Keep attending a Christian fellowship and serving the Lord diligently during this time. It is important not to separate yourself from the house of the Lord, provided your situation permits it.

Tuesday: Heb. 11: 3–12

My Insight: Faith is a powerful and mysterious concept. It can transform your life so completely that you may find it hard to believe you are the same person. However, your faith needs to be fuelled to be strong. This passage provides evidence of those whose existence has been transformed by faith. There are countless others today who can also testify.

Wednesday: Jude 20–25

My Insight: Praying in the Spirit is a strong tool as you fight for your breakthrough during this trying period. It helps direct your prayers properly. While you may be tempted to feel depressed, the Holy Spirit will guide you to pray against pertinent obstacles and keep you away from the distracting devices of the enemy.

Thursday: 2 Cor. 4: 13–18

My Insight: This passage refers to our trials as a light affliction, and the word of the Lord promises that it will work out for more glory. To accept this view appropriately, you need a measure of grace, and if you ask the Lord, he will give it to you. Otherwise, your daily coping skills will fail.

Friday: Gal. 3: 11–18

My Insight: God's word commands us to live by faith. We can't please God without it, and we can't sustain our motivation on this journey without it.

Saturday: Gal. 3: 19–29

My Insight: This passage assures you that the promise of a child is yours by divine right and determination.

Sunday: Jer. 29: 11–14

My Insight: The beauty of these verses is that they provide an assurance of a safe landing – we will laugh last. Visualise yourself carrying your baby and rejoicing at last.

Prayer Point:

I prophesy that I will fulfil the number of days of this pregnancy, in the name of Jesus.

May any person reporting my pregnancy to the evil ones receive a slap from the angels of God, in Jesus' name.

Fact: When discouraging thoughts try to enter your mind, change them to positive ones, and you will immediately benefit from the happiness you have generated for yourself.

Date:

Note / Prayers:

_____

_____

_____

_____

_____

_____

_____

_____

_____

_____

_____

_____

_____

_____

_____

_____

_____

_____

Week 30

Trials are Triggers

Trials can be a trigger for your destiny. That is, if it turns out right, it will activate a mission in your life. I listened to Oprah once, and she said that she would not change the bad things that had happened to her for anything. That surprised me until she explained why: the experiences made her into the woman she is today. Similarly, my trials crystallised my resolve to work tirelessly to help every woman conceive and give birth to her own child, by the grace of God.

Monday: Isa. 14: 24–27

My Insight: Who can change what God has ordained? Only you.

Tuesday: Isa. 46: 9–13

My Insight: The Lord has the final say. Turn a deaf ear to naysayers, and tune your frequency to His word.

Wednesday: Rom. 8: 28–31

My Insight: Print out verse 31 and keep it where you will see it daily and use it as a confession to guide you throughout this period.

Thursday: John 20: 19–29

My Insight: Everyone's level of faith is different. Some people need a sign to believe that their journey will end successfully. Others don't – they trust God to do what He promised. Do you need a sign?

Friday: Rom. 14: 7–12

My Insight: We will each need to give an account of how we handled our trials. Let yours be a good one.

Saturday: Zech. 10: 5–10

My Insight: Only God can turn a situation of barrenness into fruitfulness.

Sunday: Jas. 1: 1–8

My Insight: I cannot overemphasise the need for absolute trust and focus. Therefore, keep calm and trust God. Your testimony can nourish the hearts of millions.

Prayer Point:

Every spirit of stillbirth and threat of abortion, be consumed by fire, in the name of Jesus.

I nullify every satanic threat against my pregnancy, in Jesus' name.

Info: Motivate yourself – never let yourself be unhappy, even when you have a medical diagnosis stating that you cannot have children. Determine to get on with your life and do things that bring value to others.

Date:

Note / Prayers:

_____

_____

_____

_____

_____

_____

_____

_____

_____

_____

_____

_____

_____

_____

_____

_____

Fulfilling God's Will

God's promises are conditional, and rightly so. Sometimes, a special condition must be fulfilled before the miracle is sent. Remember Hannah? She was the apple of her husband's eye, and she had a meek and gentle soul. I believe that was why Peninah was able to upset her without retaliation. But until Hannah realised the need to make a vow – God's condition – her miracle remained firmly in His domain. Is there a condition you need to fulfil to move into the realm of answered prayer? Perhaps you need to let go of an attitude, such as anger, unforgiveness, prayerlessness, lying, stealing or something else. Is there a vow you need to make or a matter you need to make restitution for – a broken promise or covenant? Ask the Lord to shine His light on the matter, and He will reveal it to you. When He does, do not consult with others before you obey. Act immediately to resolve the matter.

Monday: Gal. 1: 15–24

My Insight: Paul obeyed God by going immediately after he received God's divine instruction to preach the gospel to all nations, not just the Jews.

Tuesday: Col. 3: 1–10.

My Insight: Check to see if you have any of the attitudes on this list that must be dealt with. Cry out to God for His mercy and grace to help in this time of need.

Wednesday: Isa. 9: 1–8

My Insight: A word of prophecy from an authentic source concerning your situation makes a difference.

Thursday: Job 40: 7–14

My Insight: Though it was a very trying period for Job, God expected this man to trust Him and took him to task over it.

Friday: Gen. 22: 1–19

My Insight: How beautiful is our story when our tests and trials end well! Let yours do this.

Saturday: Gen. 17: 1–27

My Insight: God has a plan for every trial, and it fits into His design for your life as a whole. Sometimes it brings pain, but the plan remains. Imagine a man of ninety years of age being circumcised!

Sunday: 1 Kgs. 17: 1–16

My Insight: The widow's predicament ended in a miracle because she believed a word from God.

Prayer Point:

I shall not bring forth children to sorrow, in the name of Jesus.

Every power and spirit visiting me at night and in my dreams in order to terminate my pregnancy, be destroyed in the name of Jesus.

Fact: Illness is sometimes the body's way of telling us that something is wrong in our minds.

Date:

Note / Prayers:

_____

_____

_____

_____

_____

_____

_____

_____

_____

_____

_____

_____

_____

_____

_____

_____

Week 32

Healthy Habits

Whilst waiting for a child, I tried to form some important habits, and I believe they were helpful in achieving my desired result.

- Maintaining a lifestyle of thanksgiving and praise.
- Not blaming God for the delay.
- Rejoicing passionately and genuinely with everyone who was blessed with a baby.
- Serving with joy in church and at other functions.
- Speaking targeted, diagnostic prayers aggressively and consistently, day and night.
- Giving tithes, offerings, and additional contributions to those in need.

Monday: Ps. 95: 1–8

My Insight: Praise releases newness into the atmosphere surrounding you, and it dispels discouragement.

Tuesday: Ps. 12: 15–21

My Insight: The words of the Lord are pure. No one can alter what He has said concerning you.

Wednesday: 1 Cor. 15: 50–58

My Insight: Your continued service to the Lord is noticed and is not in vain.

Thursday: Neh. 8: 1–10

My Insight: The joy of the Lord is your strength.

Friday: Heb. 5: 5–10

My Insight: Even Jesus had to go through trials, and they changed Him and validated his obedience. What are your trials accomplishing in your character?

Saturday: Luke 6: 27–38

My Insight: The waiting period is a time of sowing – repay good for evil and forgiveness for hurt; offer thanksgiving even in times of pain. These attitudes serve as a foundation for your miracle. Seek the grace of God to overcome all hurt.

Sunday: Jas. 2: 14–26

My Insight: Abraham believed God. Do you?

Prayer Point:

By the power that directed the angel Gabriel to Zachariah, let the angel of my miracle baby locate me now, in the name of Jesus.

Thank You, Lord, because I know that You have done it.

Fact: Many people do not realise how important it is to be relaxed about the process of conception. As mentioned previously, worry and stress can cause great dysfunction in the body and affect ovulation.

Date:

Note / Prayers:

_____

_____

_____

_____

_____

_____

_____

_____

_____

_____

_____

_____

_____

_____

_____

_____

_____

Week 33

Fresh Fire

Fresh fire from God is a daily affair. The Lord taught His disciples to say, "Give us this day our daily bread." Other parts of Scripture also encourage us to ask for and receive the Lord's provision daily to face the evils of that particular day. Learn to take one day at a time in your journey and cease worrying about what tomorrow holds. You need His fresh fire to focus on the challenges of the day, to glean the value of that day, to crush attacks of discouragement, and to maintain your peace. Therefore, seek the Lord for this grace on a daily basis.

Monday: Isa. 55: 6–9

My Insight: God's way of thinking is different from ours. Ask Him for a fresh perspective daily.

Tuesday: Isa. 55: 10–13

My Insight: It is a supernatural experience when God changes a source of sorrow to a source of joy. This will happen to you as you persevere in prayer.

Wednesday: Exod. 13: 20–22

My Insight: The Lord's Word will provide light during this journey. Stick with it, day and night.

Thursday: Exod. 24: 15–18

My Insight: Moses had to wait until the seventh day before God spoke. Sometimes, a word from God will take time to come – don't abort the waiting period through impatience. Wait for Him to speak, and receive His peace.

Friday: Num. 9: 15–23

My Insight: The children of Israel learned in the wilderness to follow God's leading – when to move, or when to stay in one place and pitch their tent. No matter how long or short the stay, they obeyed His signs. Similarly, it is beneficial to study how God leads you as an individual so that you will make few errors along the way.

Saturday: Ps. 50: 1–15

My Insight: The vast resources of the heavens and earth belong to the Lord. Every blessing you need is available for His children if we will pay the price required.

Sunday: Judg. 6: 12–16

My Insight: God sees you and addresses you as the finished product, not as the current victim.

Prayer Point:

O Lord, deliver me from a womb that miscarries, in Jesus' name.

I receive the power of the Holy Spirit in my womb to carry my pregnancy to the point of delivery, in the name of Jesus.

Be Encouraged: Learn about relaxation and practice it consistently. It is not a quick-fix exercise, so it will require patience to see the results.

Date:

Note / Prayers:

_____

_____

_____

_____

_____

_____

_____

_____

_____

_____

_____

_____

_____

_____

_____

_____

Colliding with the Rock

My life was stagnant until I met someone who changed my landscape forever. I was flat on my back for months – literally. When I got up again, everything had changed – my viewpoint on life and its challenges, my philosophy, my vision, my passion, my calling, and my heart. This paradigm shift made me read my Bible differently and see God in a new light. It was the beginning of my journey to breakthrough, and it taught me that there are various levels of seeing. Colliding with the Rock of Ages broke down barriers in my life and lifted me to a higher level. Ask God what you need to see to access your breakthrough.

Monday: Isa. 6: 1–5

My Insight: It took Isaiah, the prophet, several years to have a deep encounter with God.

Tuesday: 2 Cor. 5: 17

My Insight: There are different levels of life you can experience as a believer. I began life afresh after a new encounter with God. Ask God for a deeper life experience with Him to enter into your breakthrough experience.

Wednesday: Jas. 5: 13–16

My Insight: Gathering prayer from every available source is like a cloud that soaks up and finally releases moisture. Keep praying until you see your desired goal.

Thursday: Isa. 6: 6–13

My Insight: Isaiah's main source of communication was his lips, and they required purging at this encounter. What needs to be purged in your life to make you better able to fulfil your calling? Ask the Lord in prayer.

Friday: Jas. 5: 17–18

My Insight: God does not base His decision regarding whom to bless on our wealth or qualifications but on our heart, desire, faith, and determination. He does not hold our weaknesses against us.

Saturday: Jas. 5: 19–20

My Insight: This is a reminder that one of the purposes of our trials, especially after experiencing a deeper level of life, is to help others out of their situation.

Sunday: Acts 9: 1–9

My Insight: Sometimes, God must knock us down to change our viewpoint on life. Could this be an opportunity for you to experience something similar?

Prayer Point:

Everything written or assigned against my ability to bear children, wither, in the name of Jesus.

Let the power of infertility and fear in my life be destroyed, in Jesus' name.

Motivation: Write on a card incidents that make you smile so that whenever you are tempted to be depressed or unhappy, you can change your mood.

Date:

Note / Prayers:

_____

_____

_____

_____

_____

_____

_____

_____

_____

_____

_____

_____

_____

_____

_____

_____

Experiencing Breakthroughs

You must go through a process to resolve any problem, and no problem gives way without the application of principles. These principles are undergirded by the saying, "If you do what you've always done, you get what you've always gotten." Breakthroughs do not happen by accident – they have trigger points, and making the decision to change fundamental beliefs and attitudes is the key to activating them. Ask the Lord to help you discern what steps to take that will culminate in your breakthrough.

Monday: Gen. 32: 24–31

My Insight: Jacob made the decision to battle his way out of fear and bondage to the death threat hanging over his head.

Tuesday: 1 Sam. 1: 11–18

My Insight: Hannah made the decision to get out of barrenness.

Wednesday: Luke 22: 41–46

My Insight: Jesus made the decision to struggle to the bleeding point with the fear of death. He was not exempted even though He is the Son of God.

Thursday: Josh. 12: 7–24

My Insight: Joshua consistently fought and conquered several territories.

Friday: Exod. 15: 1–8

My Insight: One of God's names is Jehovah, the man of war. His children need to be like Him.

113

Saturday: 1Kgs. 18: 1–21

My Insight: Elijah constantly battled against forces of darkness in the land of Israel, despite being a prophet. He also faced personal battles against discouragement and fear.

Sunday: Exod. 7: 19–25, 8: 16–32

My Insight: Moses contended for the freedom of the children of Israel with a series of plagues against their enemies. He left Egypt in shambles from which it has failed to recover, to this day.

Prayer Point:

Every evil power appearing to me through an animal, man, or woman, be destroyed by fire, in Jesus' name.

I reject every satanic stress during my pregnancy, in Jesus' name.

Fact: Food has a direct impact on health or disease. More specifically, proper nutrition plays a powerful role in helping us overcome health threats, and there are clear and direct connections between the foods that we eat and the prevention and treatment of heart disease, high blood pressure, diabetes, and some types of cancer.

Date:

Note / Prayers:

_____

_____

_____

_____

_____

_____

_____

_____

_____

_____

_____

_____

_____

_____

_____

_____

Miracles in Disguise

Sometimes our miracles are wrapped up in the lives of others, and it is our prerogative to hunt for and discover them. Look after the people God brings your way, especially your family, people of God, and bosses or colleagues. Offer them support, encouragement, and love. Doing this will release hidden treasures and trigger words of blessing, revelation, and prophecy that can line your path to breakthrough. Take another look at Hannah's situation. Instead of railing at the High Priest when he accused her of drunkenness, she answered in humility, and he pronounced a blessing upon her which took effect as soon as it left his lips. That same month, Hannah conceived. How are you treating the people God sends your way?

Monday: 2 Kgs. 3: 11

My Insight: Elisha poured water on the hands of Elijah.

Tuesday: 2 Kgs. 5: 1–6

My Insight: The maid who waited on Naaman's wife was the source of their deliverance.

Wednesday: Matt. 27: 57–60

My Insight: Joseph of Arimathea obtained the body of Jesus from the authorities to give Him a befitting burial and grave.

Thursday: 1 Sam. 1: 12–20

My Insight: The High Priest blessed Hannah, and she conceived at the next possible opportunity.

Friday: 2 Kgs. 4: 1–7

My Insight: The prophet told the woman what to do to redeem her sons from debtors.

Saturday: 2 Kgs. 4: 17–37

My Insight: The prophet brought the Shunammite's son back to life.

Sunday: Gen. 41: 9–14

My Insight: The butler remembered Joseph and mentioned him to Pharaoh.

Prayer Point:

O Lord, help me to conquer the power of miscarriage, in Jesus' name.

O Lord, give me the wings of a great eagle to escape from miscarriage, in the name of Jesus.

Fact: Among the most common conception-related problems in women is a hormone imbalance, typically between oestrogen and progesterone. Depending on the severity, it can cause a wide range of ailments, from a temporary disruption in ovulation to a complete cessation of the menstrual period.

Date:

Note / Prayers:

_____

_____

_____

_____

_____

_____

_____

_____

_____

_____

_____

_____

_____

_____

_____

_____

_____

Week 36 B
(may be completed in same week as 36A)

Fire

Fire has diverse abilities and can be both good and evil.

Spiritual fire can:

- Help you see clearer
- Cleanse and purify you
- Destroy yokes
- Melt bondage away
- Bring clarity of thought
- Foster love for God and neighbours
- Bring speed of limbs
- Facilitate intense worship

Ask the Lord for fresh fire daily. As it accumulates, you become a purer vessel, and the anointing of breakthrough can flow through you like a current.

Monday: Judg. 16: 7–9

My Insight: Samson was empowered by the Spirit of God – who sometimes manifests as fire.

Tuesday: 1Kgs. 19: 5–8

My Insight: Elijah was empowered to travel for forty days and nights without food after an encounter with God's Spirit.

Wednesday: 1 Kgs. 18: 30–40

My Insight: The fire of God came down on Elijah's sacrifice and broke yokes of unbelief and witchcraft.

Thursday: Acts 1: 8, 2: 1–4

My Insight When the Holy Ghost baptised 120 disciples in the Upper Room, they were delivered from fear and filled with courage to witness in a hostile environment.

Friday: 2 Kgs. 1: 1–15

My Insight: The fire of God came down to consume the soldiers who sought to arrest Elijah.

Saturday: Exod. 13: 20–22

My Insight: A pillar of fire led the Israelites at night.

Sunday: Heb. 12: 22–29

My Insight: Our God is a consuming fire.

Prayer Point:

O Lord, give me a child, in the name of Jesus.

I declare that I am fruitful, and I will bring forth offspring in peace, in the name of Jesus.

Fact: When medical conditions are a result of a hormone imbalance, a change in diet can often help correct what has gone amiss.

Date:

Note / Prayers:

_____

_____

_____

_____

_____

_____

_____

_____

_____

_____

_____

_____

_____

_____

_____

Week 37

Twenty-Four-Hour Miracle

I stood in the ladies toilet at work one afternoon, staring at the mirror in shock as I noticed that my eyes had wrinkles at the sides. "O Lord," I said, "I have these wrinkles, and I'm starting to sprout grey hairs. Will I bring up a child in my old age? I cried out to the Lord in despair. "Please help me!"

The Lord heard my cry. The following month, I was pregnant.

Monday: Phil. 4: 1–7

My Insight: Be afraid of nothing.

Tuesday: 1 Kgs. 18: 41–45

My Insight: What you hear in your spirit matters for your breakthrough.

Wednesday: Luke 22: 40–45

My Insight: Jesus faced the greatest challenge of His life before facing the cross – fear of separation from His Father. As He cried out to God, His strength was restored, and He received His breakthrough: the grace He needed to pass through the fire of the Cross.

Thursday: Gen. 32: 7-–31

My Insight: Jacob was fearful for His life and prayed all night to God for deliverance. By morning, his destiny was changed.

Friday: Luke 7: 36–43

My Insight: Tears and worship are an effective combination for breakthrough

Saturday: Luke 2:36–40

My Insight: Anna was a devout woman of God. She stayed in the temple praying for all her widowed years until she saw the Messiah – her lifelong dream.

Sunday: Gen. 22: 6–14

My Insight: Abraham looked up after raising his knife to slay Isaac, and God had provided a ram for the sacrifice – because Abraham was willing to give up his son.

Prayer Point:

Every power that has swallowed up my children, return them now, in the name of Jesus.

Every foundation of miscarriage, receive the judgment of God, in the name of Jesus.

Fact: The benefits of adding fruits, vegetables, and nuts to your daily diet go far beyond protecting you from insulin resistance and fertility-related problems. These foods are a source of healthy fibre and contain many of the vitamins that affect fertility positively.

Date:

Note / Prayers:

_____

_____

_____

_____

_____

_____

_____

_____

_____

_____

_____

_____

_____

_____

_____

_____

_____

_____

Week 38

Touching Prayer

I heard my husband pray one day, "Thank You, Lord, for how You have supported us and taken care of us. Thank You for Your love for us." Wow! I was blown away by such words. I wonder how God felt.

Monday: Eph. 5: 15–20

My Insight: Our thanksgiving is more potent when it is offered up to God despite our challenging circumstances.

Tuesday: Gen. 21: 1–7

My Insight: When you praise God, remember that He keeps His word at the appointed time.

Wednesday: Luke 1: 13–25

My Insight: The Lord's word must surely come to pass.

Thursday: Luke 1: 28–35

My Insight: God can do anything to enable us able to get our breakthrough. However, he probably will not perform another immaculate conception.

Friday: Ps. 145: 20

My Insight: God has diverse ways of accomplishing His purposes.

Saturday: Ps. 18: 3–19

My Insight: Praise makes God favourable towards us – practice it often.

Sunday: Ps. 5: 1–7

My Insight: A life of disciplined worship is a requirement for breakthrough.

Prayer Point:

I command any fibroid to remove itself from my womb, in the name of Jesus.

Every low sperm count be converted to a full sperm count, in the name of Jesus.

Fact: There are two main types of carbohydrates – simple and complex. Simple ones break down very easily and release sugar into your bloodstream quickly. Complex ones are slow-burning and release sugar more slowly.

Date:

Note / Prayers:

_____

_____

_____

_____

_____

_____

_____

_____

_____

_____

_____

_____

_____

_____

_____

_____

It's Not Who Gets There First

Some people achieve milestones very fast, while others take their time to arrive at the same destination. In terms of childbearing, some conceive on the wedding night, while others may wait twenty years. Each person has a different course to chart. That is why comparing your situation to another couple's is not only unwise but dangerous. God has a plan for you which is different to the plan for your twin, sibling, or friend. Do not fall prey to keeping up with the Joneses, especially when it concerns childbearing. This will lead to foolishness and depression.

Monday: 2 Cor. 10: 12–14

My Insight: It is not wise to compare ourselves with each other.

Tuesday: Gen. 30: 1–8

My Insight: Leah and Rachel were rivals in their own home. They competed in having children.

Wednesday: Gen. 41: 46–49

My Insight: Though Rachel had only two children, one became a ruler and delivered his entire family and the nation of Israel from death during a famine.

Thursday: Exod. 20: 13

My Insight: God has ordained who should give birth to each child. Therefore, never seek to have another's portion.

Friday: Gen. 49: 22–26

My Insight: Joseph, Rachel's firstborn, became most significant among his brothers, receiving the birth right and supported two tribes – Manasseh and Ephraim.

Saturday: Gen. 29: 31–34, 30: 17–20

My Insight: Though Leah was despised, she was the mother of half of the nation of Israel.

Sunday: Luke 12: 6, 7

My Insight: Even the hairs on our heads have individual numbers in God's book; how unique are our lives?

Prayer Point:

Throughout the period of the pregnancy, I shall not be stressed. I will receive angelic ministration, in the name of Jesus.

My body, be strong to labour, in the name of Jesus.

Fact: Slow-burning carbs allow insulin adequate time to get the sugar into your cells from your bloodstream. Too many simple carbs or overloading on carbs over a long period can cause the pancreas to work too hard to release insulin adequate to clear your blood sugar.

Date:

Note / Prayers:

_____

_____

_____

_____

_____

_____

_____

_____

_____

_____

_____

_____

_____

_____

_____

_____

_____

Don't Compare Destinies

Mary was in her teens when she got pregnant with Jesus, while Elizabeth had passed menopause when she got pregnant. However, both of their sons made a significant impact on world history. John the Baptist was crucial to the plan of God and the coming of the Lord Jesus – to prepare the Jewish people's hearts for their Messiah. Jesus, Saviour of the world, has changed destinies in every generation and is set to change them in the future. Are you still comparing yourself with others? Instead, keep in mind that each person has his or her unique destiny.

Monday: Gen. 4: 1–8

My Insight: For Cain and Abel, comparison and jealousy led to murder and punishment from God.

Tuesday: Gen. 25: 25–28

My Insight: For Esau and Jacob, rivalry between the brothers – and the fact that their parents played favourites – led to multiple problems and enmity in the home.

Wednesday: Esther 1: 9–20, 2: 5–9: 17

My Insight: Consider Vashti and Esther. Two different women, given the same opportunity, handled it differently – one with apparent pride, the other with humility.

Thursday: Gen. 35: 22, 48: 12, 49: 3–4, 22–26

My Insight: In the case of Reuben and Joseph, one brother was the heir by birth, and he sold his birthright on the bed of immorality. The other had his birthright transferred to him by reason of his faithfulness to God, his forgiving nature, and his deep reverence for his father.

Friday: 1 Sam. 15: 16–23, 16: 11–13

My Insight: Look at Saul and David's situation. In the case of these two kings, one lost his kingdom through disobedience and pride, whilst the other established his kingdom through faithfulness and worship.

Saturday: 2 Kgs. 2: 11–16, 2 Kgs. 5: 20–31

My Insight: Elisha and Gehazi behaved differently: Gehazi could have been the most powerful prophet of all time, but he preferred material possessions to the power of God.

Sunday: Gal. 1: 16–17

My Insight: Peter and Paul also had different destinies. Peter did not go and preach to the Gentiles to the extent that God desired him to, so God sent Paul to do so.

Prayer Point:

O Lord, send Your heavenly nurse to minister to me throughout the period of this pregnancy, in the name of Jesus.

I shall bring forth a normal child to the glory of God, in Jesus' name.

Fact: A continuous overload of sugar in your bloodstream can cause insulin resistance, the precursor to the more serious condition of Type 2 diabetes and a cause of fertility-related problems for some women.

Date:

Note / Prayers:

_____

_____

_____

_____

_____

_____

_____

_____

_____

_____

_____

_____

_____

_____

_____

_____

_____

_____

Week 41

Perfect Obedience

In August 1985 a Boeing 747 took off on a routine flight, carrying 524 people from Japan. Within minutes, there was an explosion, and the pilots lost control of the plane. By sheer skill, they kept it in the air for thirty minutes until they could no longer do so, and it crashed in the Japanese mountains. For fourteen hours, no help was rendered because of the politics on the ground. An investigation later showed that the cause of the explosion was an insufficient number of brackets used to repair a fault in the plane's wing some years before. A single row of brackets led to the loss of 520 lives – but how do you quantify the loss?

Little foxes that spoil the vineyards in our lives follow the same pattern. A one-night stand leads to a lifetime of regret – one indiscretion in an otherwise perfect record. Remember David's story? One incident of disobedience to the Most High can lead to several years of sorrow and pain. Review your decisions in light of this information and revisit your moral code in preparation for victory in this battle. Our lives must be holy and without blemish. The importance of living right can never be overemphasised.

Monday: Song of Solomon 2: 15

My Insight: Little foxes – like small problems that have a large effect – spoil the vines.

Tuesday: 2 Sam. 22: 21–27

The need for righteousness in our lives cannot be overstressed.

Wednesday: Luke 8: 14–16

We must continually strive for perfection in all areas of our lives.

Thursday: 1 Chron. 16: 28–34

A life of constant reverence for God is important in achieving victory.

Friday: Gen. 39: 9

A life characterised by the desire to please God attracts favour from both Him and people.

Saturday: 1 Pet. 1: 18–19

Sin can result in spiritual spots and blemishes which muddy the waters of salvation if not removed by Jesus.

Sunday: 1 Sam. 15: 22

Never take God's Word for granted – this leads to trouble.

Prayer Point:

O Lord, deliver me from the spirit of error, in the name of Jesus.

I condemn the hold of mismanagement of my health through wrong medical advice or wrong medication, in Jesus' name.

Fact: Insulin is a hormone. Its production and release are part of a finely tuned network of balanced hormonal activity. Therefore, a diet high in simple carbs can disrupt that network and interrupt the release of your eggs.

Date:

Note / Prayers:

_____

_____

_____

_____

_____

_____

_____

_____

_____

_____

_____

_____

_____

_____

Week 42

Mirror Image

A lady prayed for her second child to look like her husband because her first looked so much like her that the spouse felt left out. God honoured her request, and the resemblance was uncanny! Have you remembered to ask God for the kind of children you want – including the sex, facial features, character, heart, personality, and destiny? God has the final say, but you can ask for what you want, and He will grant your request as it pleases Him. Please note that a healthy child who does not have all the characteristics you desire is of great worth and is God's chosen answer to your prayer. Remember the daughters Job was blessed with after his trials. On the other hand, beauty is vain without a good heart, so there is need for balance in our requests. A heart that fears God is paramount.

Monday: Job 42: 12–16

My Insight: Job's daughters were the prettiest in the land.

Tuesday: Exod. 2: 2, Num. 12: 3–10

My Insight: Moses was a good-looking child and the meekest man on earth.

Wednesday: 1 Sam. 16: 10–13

My Insight: David was good-looking and had a heart after God.

Thursday: 2 Sam. 14: 25–26, 2 Sam. 15: 1–6.

My Insight: Absalom was fair to look at but had an evil heart.

Friday: 2 Sam. 11: 2–5, 24–27

My Insight: Bathsheba was breathtakingly beautiful, but she allowed the king to have sex with her and didn't speak up when he killed her husband.

Saturday: Ezek. 28: 17–19

My Insight: Beauty can bring pride as in Lucifer's case; therefore, it is not the most important feature in a child.

Sunday: Prov. 31: 30

My Insight: A heart that fears God is the priority.

Prayer Point:

Cervix, close up, and let there be no contractions or dilation before the nine-month period is complete, in the name of Jesus.

I receive power from on high to bring forth a child, in the name of Jesus.

Fact: Androgens, including testosterone, are male hormones. Normally, the ovaries produce small amounts of testosterone. However, when the level of insulin is consistently high, ovaries increase the production. This depletes the production of oestrogen, impacting egg production and leading to temporary infertility.

Date:

Note / Prayers:

_____

_____

_____

_____

_____

_____

_____

_____

_____

_____

_____

_____

_____

_____

_____

_____

_____

_____

_____

Another Day, Another Miracle

Every new day should bring you fresh hope. How do you know which one will bring the promise you await? Listen to the pitter-patter of rain on the roof, the sounds of birds tweeting and frogs croaking, the cornucopia of early-morning noises, and cars starting and trains moving into motion as the world awakes. Give thanks to the Lord for a new opportunity to receive from the abundance He has prepared for you and the chance to sing His praise. Each day, you can make amends for the mistakes of yesterday and thank Him for a fresh crop of miracles coming your way. A new morning is another chance to pick up where you left off the day before with more laughter, more joy, more peace, and more of God in your life. It is another opportunity for your baby to come.

Thank You, Lord!

Monday: Ps. 105: 1–5

My Insight: Give thanks to the Lord – experiencing His kindness makes the journey more bearable.

Tuesday: 1 Kgs. 17: 1–7

My Insight: As surely as the Lord lives, your desires shall be granted in His perfect will.

Wednesday: Jer. 29: 12–14

Call upon Him, and He will answer you.

Thursday: Jer. 33: 1–3

He will show you great and mighty things that you do not yet know.

Friday: Prov. 21: 29–31

The horse is prepared for the day of battle, but victory is from the Lord.

Saturday: Eccles. 11: 6

Sow your seeds of faith at all times, as you never know which one will come to maturity.

Sunday: 1 Cor. 15: 58

Abound in service to others.

Prayer Point:

I break the arm of the wicked that may be exercising evil against me, in the name of Jesus.

Holy Spirit, envelop me and overshadow me throughout the period of this pregnancy, in the name of Jesus.

Act: If high levels of sugar in the bloodstream are maintained, this can lead to a more prolonged and increasingly complex form of infertility.

Date:

Note / Prayers:

_____

_____

_____

_____

_____

_____

_____

_____

_____

_____

_____

_____

_____

_____

_____

_____

Week 44

Wait with Wisdom

Use your waiting time wisely – you may never have a focused time like this again. Prepare yourself for your coming miracle. After having waited so long, you need to give this baby your best. Read all you can about babies and how best to look after them. One book I recommend is *What to Expect When You're Expecting*, by Heidi Murkoff and Sharon Mazel, in its fourth edition at the time of this writing. This book explains everything you need to know during the full nine months of pregnancy and more. Read it to reduce surprises, avoid accidents, and remove fear and misconceptions. Make sure to do all that you can to provide the best care for your child spiritually and physically and to make the wait worthwhile.

Monday: Ps. 90.12:

My Insight: Teach us to number our days.

Tuesday: Eph. 5: 14–17

My Insight: Time passes quickly, so use it well.

Wednesday: 2 Tim. 2: 15–17

My Insight: Study to show yourself approved of God.

Thursday: Luke 14: 28–32

My Insight: What person trying to build a house will not sit down to consider if he or she has enough to complete the project?

Friday: Phil. 4: 13

My Insight: Learning the skills of motherhood is not easy, but God's grace is sufficient for the willing mum.

Saturday: 1 Sam. 2: 19–20; Prov. 31: 27–28

My Insight: Others have excelled in motherhood, and so can you.

Sunday: 1 Sam. 2: 21

My Insight: The Lord will give you a child. He knows you can take good care of him or her. Ask for God's grace.

Prayer Point:

I will not labour in vain or bring forth to trouble, in Jesus' name.

As I build, I will inhabit, and as I plant, I shall eat, in Jesus' name

Fact: Polycystic Ovarian Syndrome (PCOS) is an insulin-related fertility disorder which manifests as eggs that are not ovulated as well as other symptoms. The facts given in previous weeks about hormone imbalances and excess sugars explain how this can happen.

Date:

Note / Prayers:

_____

_____

_____

_____

_____

_____

_____

_____

_____

_____

_____

_____

_____

_____

_____

_____

_____

_____

Break the Mould

Anything you do that breaks the mould elevates you to the status of a teacher. Oprah says (7),

"I've come to believe that each of us has a personal calling that's as unique as a fingerprint - and that the best way to succeed is to discover what you love and then find a way to offer it to others in the form of service, working hard..."

In my words, if you do something, working hard to make it different and unique to your call, and it yields outstanding results, it gives you the opportunity to teach many people. So, go on and break the mould! Do something differently and change your location or angle; change your Consultant if you have to – listen to a different mentor. Do something daring, and make sure you pray!

Monday: Gen. 33: 8–11

My Insight: Esau managed to turn his destiny around from a servant to an owner of cattle.

Tuesday: Gen. 35: 9–15

My Insight: Jacob changed his destiny.

Wednesday: Neh. 12: 43–47

My Insight: Nehemiah changed the story of his people.

Thursday: Dan. 1: 21, 6: 28

My Insight: Daniel served three kings successfully.

Friday: Esther 9: 12–23

My Insight: Esther changed her story and that of her nation.

Saturday: 1 Chron. 4: 9–10

My Insight: Jabez was more honourable than his brethren.

Sunday: Eph. 3: 1–9

My Insight: Paul set a record that was hard to beat even among the disciples who walked with Jesus.

Prayer Point:

I as well as the children the Lord has given me are to demonstrate signs and wonders, in the name of Jesus.

Thank you, God, for answering my prayers.

Fact: A group of Harvard researchers analysed data from a massive nationwide American Nurses Project. They found that out of 18,000 women, those who consumed a diet high in simple carbohydrates were 92 per cent more likely to have ovulation-related infertility concerns than those whose diet was not so high in sugar content.

Date:

Note / Prayers:

_____

_____

_____

_____

_____

_____

_____

_____

_____

_____

_____

_____

_____

_____

_____

Week 46

Love Is Not Enough

Love is not enough to sustain a marriage, especially one going through the pressures of childlessness. Many couples have thrown in the towel as a result of the trials, anxiety, stress, and strain they experience. Here are some measures to keep a marriage from breaking.

- Practice consistent prayer for the marriage. You can pray together with your husband or choose a prayer partner with whom you do not need to share intimate details, but ensure that you cover the relationship in prayer.
- Monitor lines of communication – are you really talking to each other? Communication happens on different levels and is only effective if you are speaking from the heart, sharing your innermost thoughts, opinions, and feelings.
- Do not take each other for granted. People make the common error of appreciating everyone outside our home and losing our temper with the weaknesses of our immediate family members.
- Be fair – don't be too hard on each other or yourself.

Monday: 1 Sam. 1: 1–5

My Insight: Elkanah communicated with his wife and encouraged her regularly.

Tuesday: 1 Sam. 1: 8–9

My Insight: Despite Elkanah's patience and understanding, he could not fill the void Hannah felt.

Wednesday: Judg. 13: 8–15

My Insight: Samson's mother ran to get her supportive husband when the angel appeared.

Thursday: Gen. 30: 14–17

My Insight: Jacob's family situation was tense with strife.

Friday: Gen. 33: 1–2

My Insight: The tension previously mentioned bred all sorts of negative emotions in Jacob's family.

Saturday: Gen. 25: 21–25

My Insight: Isaac was prayerful at the time Rebecca most needed his support.

Sunday: Jas. 3: 16–17

My Insight: Avoid quarrelling, especially at times when you are trusting God for a breakthrough.

Prayer Point:

Any material in my body from the dark kingdom that is being used against my ability to conceive, I bring it into the light, in the name of Jesus.

I break all ungodly soul ties with sexual partners of the past, in the name of Jesus.

Fact: It was discovered that some women who consistently snacked on foods like white bread, pasta, white rice, cookies, and potatoes not only had their ability to conceive hampered, it blocked them from getting pregnant at all!

Date:

Note / Prayers:

_____

_____

_____

_____

_____

_____

_____

_____

_____

_____

_____

_____

_____

_____

_____

_____

Week 47

God of the Spectacular

When God does a spectacular work in your life, you have a testimony to share with others. It will:

- Repair shattered dreams
- Encourage the weary
- Renew the strength of many
- Turn back the rebellious
- Wipe away the tears of the downcast
- Give someone a ray of hope in a storm

It pleases God to be good to you and put a smile on your face!

Monday: Gen. 21: 1–7

Sarah's Story

Tuesday: Exod. 15: 1–19

Moses' Song

Wednesday: 1 Sam. 2: 1–10

Hannah's Song

Thursday: Ps. 23: 1–6

David's Psalm

Friday: Luke 1: 46–56

Mary's Worship

Saturday: Luke 1: 57–66

Elizabeth's Testimony

Sunday: Luke 1: 67–80

Zechariah's Prophecy

Prayer Point:

As I build, I will inhabit; as I plant, I shall eat, in Jesus' name.

I refuse to consider the doctors' negative report, in the name of Jesus.

Fact: The American Dietetic Association confirmed that fibre is an essential element for controlling blood sugar and losing weight – two factors that play an important role in fertility.

Date:

Note / Prayers:

_____

_____

_____

_____

_____

_____

_____

_____

_____

_____

_____

_____

_____

_____

_____

_____

_____

Week 48

Receiving a Name

You need to be prepared for your child in every department. Have you thought of a name yet? God often names children and can do so well in advance of their birth (e.g., Jesus and John). Be sure to give your child the name God provides, as He does so for a reason. When David named his son Solomon, God had already given the boy another name – Jedidiah, meaning "Beloved of God". In addition, the child's name will dictate his or her destiny in life.

God also renamed some people in the Bible: Abram to Abraham, Sarai to Sarah, Jacob to Israel, and Cephas to Peter. If God considers a name so important, believing families ought to seek Him regarding the name of their child. Put quality time and prayer into the choice, and the Lord will reward you fully with His own choice. Nothing can be more fulfilling.

Monday: Gen. 17: 5–14

Abram became Abraham.

Tuesday: Gen. 17: 15–21

Sarai became Sarah.

Wednesday: Gen. 32: 24–30

Jacob became Israel.

Thursday: Esther 2: 7–10

Hadassah was known as Queen Esther

Friday: 2 Sam. 12: 24–25

Solomon was loved by God, who named him Jedidiah.

Saturday: Matt. 1: 18–25

His name is Jesus.

Sunday: Luke 1: 13–17

His name is John.

Prayer Point:

Every violent miscarriage, stop permanently, in the name of Jesus.

I reject every manifestation of fever during my pregnancy, in the name of Jesus.

Use the following guidance for your fertility diet:

1. Eat twenty grams or more of fibre daily.
2. Ensure that a type of whole grain is the first ingredient in breads and muffins.
3. Choose whole fruit instead of fruit juices, and include at least one with your breakfast.
4. Add more beans to your diet, as they are full of complex carbs and plant proteins.

Date:

Note / Prayers:

_____

_____

_____

_____

_____

_____

_____

_____

_____

_____

_____

_____

_____

_____

_____

_____

_____

If You Can See It, You Can Have It

God is a great Teacher, Mentor, and Father. He instructed Abraham to look at the stars and the land as far as his sight could reach to help him understand his future. Several generations later, I stand as a fulfilment of that promise – I am a spiritual descendant of Abraham.

God operates on the principle of vision and revelation: if you perceive it, it's yours. On two occasions, my husband and I needed to move house, as our living quarters were too small. In the first instance, I breathed the air in a particular neighbourhood, and my heart said, "This is where I want to live." A few years later, we moved into a house a street away from where I took that first breath. After some time there, I could not pray out loud because the noise disturbed the neighbours. We prayed about it, and this time we landed in a home where no one could hear us pray no matter how loud. If you can see something in your spirit, ask God, and you will get it if it is according to His will.

Monday: Gen. 15: 5–16

Lift up your eyes and see.

Tuesday: 2 Kgs. 4: 14–17

As surely as the Lord lives, by this time next year …

Wednesday: 2 Kgs. 3: 15–20

Bring me a minstrel.

Thursday: 1 Kgs. 17: 1–7

As surely as the Lord lives, before whom I stand ...

Friday: John 7: 17

He will teach His doctrine to those who fear Him.

Saturday: Gal. 3: 13–14

Those of us who were classified as Gentiles in times past can now receive the blessing of Abraham.

Sunday: Mark 9: 17–27

If you believe, you will see His glory.

Prayer Point:

This year, all of those who have looked down on me because of my condition shall laugh with me, in the name of Jesus.

By the power in the blood of Jesus, my expectations shall not be cut off, in the name of Jesus.

This week's steps for your fertility diet:

1. Switch to whole-wheat pasta
2. Choose a high-fibre breakfast cereal such as bran flakes or oatmeal.
3. Reduce your intake of simple carbohydrates – those made with white flour (e.g., bread, cakes, cookies, pies).
4. Where possible, substitute these with carbs made from whole grains.

Date:

Note / Prayers:

_____

_____

_____

_____

_____

_____

_____

_____

_____

_____

_____

_____

_____

_____

Now

When I now hold my son in my arms, I am filled with wonder, gratitude, fulfilment, and hope:

That I finally have my own child

That he is so amazing

That he depends on me

That he loves me

That God remembered me

That God rewarded me

That God loves me

That God kept His promise!

Monday: Ps. 136: 1–29

Give thanks unto the Lord, for He is good.

Tuesday: Ps. 118: 31–39

I have a God who never fails.

Wednesday: Ps. 84: 1–12

No good thing will He withhold from those who walk uprightly.

Thursday: Ps. 113: 1–9

He makes the barren woman become a mother of many.

Friday: Ps. 126: 1–6

He makes His children laugh out loud.

Saturday: Isa. 40: 25–31

He gives strength to the weak.

Sunday: Ps. 46: 1–7

He is a very present help in trouble.

The next fertility diet steps:

1. Try to keep up your five-a-day fruits and vegetables.
2. Include one fruit and one vegetable with every meal
3. Try to eat one serving of red or blue-coloured berries every day.
4. Aim for three meals a week that consist solely of fruits, vegetables, and a high-fibre carbohydrate.

Date:

Note / Prayers:

_____

_____

_____

_____

_____

_____

_____

_____

_____

_____

_____

_____

_____

_____

_____

_____

_____

In the Beginning

I had asked the Lord with tears in my eyes, "When will I be able to sing like this? When will I hold my own child in my arms? When will I sing with such transparent joy, O God?" Now, forty months on, I have tears in my eyes again – this time, they are tears of joy for answered prayer.

The following scriptures are some of my favourites:

"O You who hear prayer, to You all flesh will come" (Ps. 65: 2, NKJV).

"Weeping may endure for a night, but joy comes in the morning" (Ps. 30: 5, NKJV).

"Behold what manner of love the Father has bestowed on us, that we should be called children of God" (1 John 3: 1, NKJV).

"For I know the thoughts that I think toward you, thoughts of peace and not of evil, to give you a future and a hope" (Jer. 29: 11, NKJV).

"And you will seek me and find me, when you search for me with all your heart" (Jer. 29: 13, NKJV).

"The Lord is my Shepherd; I shall not want" (Ps. 23:1, KJV).

"He sent His Word, and healed them, and delivered them from their destructions" (Ps. 107: 20, KJV).

Guidance for your fertility diet (continued):

1. When ordering pizza, skip the extra cheese. Choose a vegetable topping like tomatoes or mushrooms instead.

164

2. When you crave a cookie or cake, eat a piece of fruit first – the craving will most likely pass.
3. Switch white potatoes with a high-fibre, slowly digesting carb, such as cauliflower or yams.
4. Remember, the brighter the colour of your fruits and vegetables, the more nutrients you are typically getting.

Date:

Note / Prayers:

_____

_____

_____

_____

_____

_____

_____

_____

_____

_____

_____

_____

_____

_____

_____

_____

_____

_____

Week 52

I Will Praise the Lord

Declare each day this week a day for praise and worship. You could, for example, praise God for a minimum of thirty minutes daily in two separate sessions, one each in the morning and evening.

Date:

Note / Prayers:

_____

_____

_____

_____

_____

_____

_____

_____

_____

_____

_____

_____

_____

_____

_____

_____

_____

Prayers for Daily or Weekly Use

Father, every plant You did not plant in my body and in my family uproot IJN.

Father, use me to put an end to every form of barrenness in my family IJN.

Father, give me a revelation of my destiny.

Father, whatever I need to overcome, please give to me now.

Father, deliver me from all troubles and sorrows.

Father, give me the grace to pay the price for my greatness.

Father, any decision that will make me a failure, do not allow me to take it.

Father, make my life a living testimony.

Let Your voice be clear to me IJN.

Let me enjoy clarity of purpose and the leading of the Holy Ghost.

Lord, cause me to always worship You in Spirit and in Truth.

I receive grace to labour on the Word and Prayer.

Lord Jesus, my life is in Your hands, please build me according to Your original design.

Every weakness in the foundation of my life, Father, strengthen it with Your mighty hand.

Father, make me a world changer to Your glory and praise, before I die!

I refuse to be an abandoned project in the hands of God.

Father, let those who have written me off be forced to submit to me in this season IJN.

Lord, let my glory and my star be respected throughout the world IJN.

Father, in this particular year, set Your table of accomplishment before me.

Father, I decree let the Heaven over me be opened right now IJN.

Father, I decree by Your authority, let the strongman that is against my breakthrough be disgraced IJN.

Confessions for Daily or Weekly Use

I declare, according to the word of God, that the Lord shall perfect everything concerning me. The Lord who has started His good work of creation in me will complete it (Phil. 1: 6).

By the power in the blood of the Lord Jesus Christ, I confess that my pregnancy is perfect, in the name of Jesus. Every part of my body shall function perfectly to form the baby, in Jesus' name. My blood shall circulate effectively.

Everything that passes from me to the baby for its development shall be perfect, in Jesus' name. I confess that I am strong – weakness is not my lot, in the name of Jesus. I will not have morning sickness or vomiting for any other reason in my pregnancy, in the name of Jesus. I reject cramps, varicose veins, and backaches, because Jesus Christ has borne all my sicknesses. I refuse constipation, anaemia, vitamin and mineral deficiencies, swollen hands and feet, hypertension, convulsions, and diabetes in the mighty name of Jesus. My urine will remain normal, in the name of Jesus (Ps. 103: 3–5). I confess that the activities of those who eat flesh and drink blood will not prosper in my life, in the name of Jesus. I refuse and reject all negative dreams, visions, prophecies, and imaginations, in the name of Jesus.

I confess God's promise in Exod. 23: 26 that I shall not have a miscarriage, abnormal bleeding, or malformation of the baby, in Jesus' name. I shall be a joyous mother. My womb is fruitful – I am a fruitful vine by the side of our house. My children are like olive plants around our table. As the baby grows, every aspect of his or her formation and development shall be perfect, in Jesus' name.

I also confess that I shall not suffer from any nausea, irritation, headaches, or internal or external pain because I am healed by the stripes of Jesus.

I tread on sickness and all the agents of the devil. My body is the temple of the Holy Spirit, and I have the life and health of Christ in me. The sun of righteousness has arisen, conquering sickness, pain, and Satan. There is healing in in His wings for me. God's will for my baby and me is to prosper and be in good health. God is at work in me now to will and to do His good pleasure. The Holy Spirit is flowing in me and perfecting all that pertains to my baby's formation, in Jesus' name.

I declare that every disease and germ shall die now, in Jesus' name. Nothing that enters my body through the mouth shall harm me or my baby, in Jesus' name. God's word says, "If I drink any deadly thing, it shall not harm me." I confess that as I go to deliver my baby, the Lord will direct on the medical staff regarding what care best suits me and the baby, in Jesus' name.

My pregnancy is established in righteousness. I am far from oppression. Therefore, I shall not fear because no terror shall come near me. No evil shall befall me or my baby, and no plague shall come near my dwelling place or my family.

The Lord shall fulfil the number of days for my pregnancy. I shall not have a premature baby, but a fully grown one. My baby shall come out alive, strong, and healthy, because nothing shall harm my young. I am fearfully and wonderfully made. My pelvis is wide enough to allow my baby to pass through, in the name of Jesus.

I also confess, according to Isa. 43, that when I pass through the water, the Lord will be with me. If go through the river, it shall not overtake me, and if I walk through the fire, I shall neither be burnt nor scorched. Therefore, I confess that I shall pass through delivery without any pain or hurt, in Jesus' name.

The Lord shall take away every sickness of pregnancy and childbearing and accompanying complications, according to Deut. 7: 14–15. I shall not fear because I have been redeemed from the curse of the law – the curse of bringing forth in agony (Gal. 4).

I boldly confess Isa. 66: 7: before I travail, I will give birth, and before any pain comes, my baby will be delivered. Moreover, according to 1 Tim. 2: 15, I will be saved in childbearing because I continue in faith, love, and holiness with self-control.

I confess that I shall go to the delivery room confidently, in Jesus' name. The Lord has given me perfect peace because my mind rests on Him. My trust is in the Lord, and Jehovah God is my everlasting strength.

According to Ps. 118: 17, I confess that I shall neither die in childbirth and neither shall my baby suffer death. We shall both live to declare the works of the Lord, in Jesus' name. My cervix shall be fully dilated and the canal wide enough to allow the baby to pass through with ease. The delivery shall be perfect, in Jesus' name. No evil shall befall me or my baby. No weapon of the devil that is fashioned against me or my baby shall prosper, in Jesus' name.

The Lord is the strength of my life; of whom shall I be afraid (Ps. 27: 1)? He is my deliverer, my God, my buckler, and the horn of my salvation. The Load is all I need to take me through delivery on that day. He will strengthen the bars of my gate, and He has blessed my children within me. Therefore, through the Lord, I shall do valiantly. I will live to be the happy mother of my baby. None of us shall see death, in Jesus' name. I refuse the possibility of prolonged labour and reject all pain from the devil during labour and afterwards.

I look forward to the rearing of my children after birth. I confess that we shall bring them up in the way of the Lord. The children will grow up to know and love the Lord from their youth. I also confess that the Lord shall supply all our needs during pregnancy and those of the babies after their delivery, in Jesus' name.

Glory be to the name of the Lord, because I shall have what I ask in Jesus' name.

Testimonies

- I got married in May 2003 and I naturally assumed that I would get pregnant immediately. However, this was not to be so. I went to see a doctor friend of mine and she examined me, telling me I had fibroids and referred me to run a couple of tests. By the time the results came I was told I had multiple fibroids and they were in the womb. This was the beginning of my medical sojourn. I went to see a couple of other doctors and I remember one of them said categorically that before I could get pregnant, I would need to have surgery because there was no way the baby would grow with fibroids and that even if I took all the Clomids in this world, I wouldn't get pregnant. Another doctor I went to see told me that my Prolactin was too high and I was placed on medication. After 3 months of using the medication, nothing happened. I was referred to a gynaecologist in LUTH (Lagos University Teaching Hospital, Nigeria) who told me my cycle was anovulatory - which meant that I wasn't ovulating. I was also told to chart my cycle using my temperature so that I could determine when I ovulated. All this while, I was still taking Clomid and folic acid religiously. I also went to see another doctor who told me that I had cysts in my ovary and only Clomid could rectify it.

- This really got to me and that night I cried all the way home. After a lot of consultations with different doctors, my husband and I agreed that I should go and have the fibroids removed. The surgery happened on July 10, 2006 and I was given a clean bill of health. I had an HSG (Hysterosalpingogram – an X-ray test that looks at the inside of the uterus and fallopian tubes and the area around them) done and my Fallopian tubes and ovaries could be seen during the X-ray. I naturally expected to get pregnant immediately but this also didn't happen. At this point, I must

175

mention that each time I went to God in prayer, He would give me a Word concerning my situation and I would write it down. It was very tough in the face of it all. He had told me specifically that I would have a son (Deuteronomy 6 v 20) and He had given me a name for him. Oluwatobiloba. There was even a time I told God that if He didn't want me to have any children, He should let me know now so I would stop praying about it. God indeed is a merciful God and His ways are not our ways. In 2008, my husband and I agreed to try IVF and we went to one of the clinics in Lagos. I ran some tests, and the doctor told me that with the result and my age, it would be best for me to use donor eggs because they didn't think my eggs were viable. This was to say the least, devastating. I cried all the way home and I was wondering if this was part of God's plans for me. My mind went to Sarah who gave Hagar to Abraham so she could have children through her and I thought is that my own case too?

We tried another IVF clinic in Lagos and I was told that yes my eggs weren't exactly fantastic but they would work with it. This was like music to my ears. However, none of the cycles I had there came to fruition. At different times, none of the eggs fertilized. At this point in time, I was really despondent because I wondered where the children would come from. At this time, we decided that we weren't going to seek medical attention anymore. Let things just take its course.

In 2010, we went on vacation to the US and registered in an IVF clinic in Atlanta. I was told to run some tests and send the results back to them, which I did. In 2011, I had to go back to the US for another surgery to remove one of my fallopian tubes, because it was discovered that there was fluid in it. My family was very supportive all through this time. I remember that my brothers almost quarrelled with me for not wanting to see any doctor in the US. Sometime during my quest for a baby, I was convicted by the Holy Spirit that I had put my want over and above God.

This reduced me to tears because I realized that I had neglected my fellowship with God. I also needed to answer a pertinent question - if God didn't give me any children, would I still worship him? It was a very tough question to answer but once I could, I realized that He would still be God and He is sovereign.

In October 2011, I went back to the US to start the IVF procedure. I must say at this point in time that I had been praying for God's will concerning it and He gave a word - Psalms 115 & 116. It was then I knew that God had already gone ahead of us. I started the procedure on October 30, 2011 and 4 of the eggs fertilized. On November 30, 2011, one egg was transferred and on December 9, 2011 I had a pregnancy test done and it was positive. Throughout the 9 months of pregnancy, I didn't experience any problem despite the fact that I was 'labelled' high risk. The Word that God gave in psalm 115 became my mantra. Each day I would take a verse and pray and meditate on it. However, I know that God had already purposed in His heart what He would do.On August 9, 2012, at the age of 45, I gave birth to a baby boy - Oghenebrume Oluwatobiloba who is almost 2 years of age now

I would like to tell everyone that God is faithful in spite of it all. He says weeping may endure for a night but joy comes in the morning. Hold on to the Word of God, because that is your only anchor. Make friends with the Holy Spirit because He is the only One who can tell you the message for now. Love God, develop a relationship with Him. During my 9 years of waiting, I developed my relationship with Him and that was what held me.

Every Word that He speaks to you, write it down and meditate on it because it gives hope and direction.

Be specific in your prayers, don't generalize. Search the Scriptures to back your requestBe open to all options that God has made available - it may be IVF, adoption etc. Lastly, it is very important that you pray for the husband that God has ordained for you.

OLABISI, NIGERIA

• We got married in Feb 2008 and agreed to wait for a while before starting a family. I remember a conversation with a family friend who asked us what we were waiting for to which we replied we just were not ready. He then asked what we would do when we were eventually ready.

We started trying from then on, praying fasting and believing month in month out and after about 2 years we decided to seek medical advice.

The news was devastating and we were advised that the only way was medical intervention. We still kept on believing God and asking Him to lead us- doing it His own way.

We tried two IVF cycles which failed and after then we got discouraged going down that route. Despite all this the Word kept coming that we would have our own children and this strengthened our faith.

We kept on holding on to scriptures such as Psalm 127:3; Jer 32:27 and my favourite was Matt 7:7 which we constantly quoted to God s hearing.

We also sowed into other children's lives and believed God for our own. During Christmas of 2012, my husband woke me up around 5.30am and told me that we need to start praise and worship, and I asked him why, and he said God has done it for us...that he dreamed that I was pregnant....I believed him...so we danced to His glory by faith. So in the morning, he quickly went to buy the pregnancy kit, I used one of them and the result was negative. We were both down and he later told me he had asked the Holy Spirit why didn't it happen as revealed in the dream and the response was we would rejoice on our next cycle, so he kept the second pregnancy kit which we later used to His glory.

After about a year of not going through any treatments, my husband was speaking to his friend of blessed memory who was also a Pastor and he said we shouldn't be discouraged and we should take the leap of faith, that by the end of that year we would carry our baby in our arms.

It looked like a tall order, but we did and to the glory of the cycle worked, the pregnancy was hitch free and 10 months later, our beautiful daughter Oluchi Oreoluwa Ruby was born on the 22nd Nov 2013 at 11.13pm

For anyone reading this and still waiting for God, keep holding on. His Word NEVER fails. At the right time He will surely deliver your bundle of joy into your arms. Believe His Word and not what man says about your situation. You will surely look back and the joy that comes with the breakthrough He brings will make up for all the difficult times you have experienced regarding this.

D O., UK

• I was twelve weeks into my pregnancy when they discovered a cyst on my ovary. The doctors said that they needed to perform invasive surgery, and I would lose the baby. I was distraught, but I prayed for God to have mercy on me and my child, and He heard my voice. The doctors carried out the surgery, and I gave up hope. To my utter delight, when the scan results were reviewed, my baby was alive! My daughter is gorgeous.

NANA, LONDON

- I had one healthy child and was pregnant with my second when I started to bleed at twenty-six weeks. The blood was so much that the doctors didn't know what to do. I was very confused but asked my church family to pray for me. When the bleeding subsided, the doctors were prepared for a D&C (dilation and curettage) to remove the retained products of conception. After a chance reminder to perform a scan before proceeding, the pregnancy was intact. My son was born at thirty-eight weeks. To God be the glory!

HANNAH, LONDON

- I waited on the Lord for 17 years 9 months

During my waiting period, I did the following:

Prayed CONTINOUSLY, with a strong faith in The Lord, trusting in the Lord's unfailing love.

Blessed other mothers with babies with gifts Eccl 11 v 1-6.'

Attended naming ceremonies joyfully, believing my own time will come.

Always gave gifts to new babies.

Loved children and took care of them.

Attended prayer meetings, deliverance programmes, and having a dedicated private fasting /prayer day Lk 18 v 1, Heb 10 v 25.

Prayed, thanking God all the time for my situation, knowing He will glorify Himself Ps 48 v 1-2. Served God with my whole heart saying like ESTHER 'if I perish, I perish'. Esth 4 v 16b.

Studied the word of God, knowing it by heart 2 Tim 2. 15-16, 2 Tim 3.16-17.

Shopped for babies' clothes, buying and keeping them in faith.

The trigger was the fact one was hurt by spiteful comments and asking God to fight for us and prove He is our God. An unceasing faith that He would do it. Ex 14.14

My encouragement to those still waiting on The Lord is Never Give up on God. Hold on trust God, believe and use His Word and stand on His promises – Ecc 3.11. Live a righteous life. Do not ask for help from unbelievers - 2 Cor 6.14

Know your God and serve him faithfully.

There is honour in the place of service – Lk 1:5-8

ANN ARAMIDE IBIKUNLE

NOTTINGHAM, UK

- We waited 12 years to conceive. We fasted, prayed and we believed in God for a miracle. We had faith and we added work to our faith. We were thoroughly investigated by visiting several specialists to find out what the problem was. The specialists advised that we did IVF and we carried out the procedure in two continents nine times altogether. To the glory of God we have two daughters today.

- At the point when I was getting discouraged and doubting if we would ever conceive, God gave me a girl's name after three days of dry fasting. We conceived our first daughter with the next IVF cycle. I believe it was just the time, the way God had planned it. Fasting, praying and believing that God will answer your prayer are a given. It is very important that the couple visit an infertility specialist, so that they have a diagnosis and a plan of action. Also educate yourself about your diagnosis, the internet is filled with a lot of information on infertility, do a lot of research so you can go to the best specialist in the field. A good website to visit is www.ivfconnections.com. Read books on infertility nutrition. I read that the African yam and Olive oil are very good for fertility. Never give up, always be hopefully and hold on to the promise of God for you.

F.S.T. USA

Bibliography

1. Enoch Adeboye, Father of Nations, Rebecca Bible-Davids

    Published in 2009 by Biblos Publishers – London, Johannesburg, North Carolina

2. The Overflow (with Prayer Points), E. A. Adeboye

    Published in 2013 by Freedom Press, Ibadan, Nigeria

3. Prayer Passport to crush Oppression, Dr D. K. Olukoya

    Published in 2006 by Mountain of Fire & Miracles Ministries Press House, Lagos, Nigeria

4. Getting Pregnant: The new fertility diet guide, N Lauersen & C Bouchez

    Published in 2009 by Ivy League Press, New York

5. Forgotten secrets of natural conception: How your mind affects your fertility,

    M Pangrazzi. Published in 2011 by Andrews UK Ltd

6. http://www.nhs.uk/conditions/pregnancy-and-baby/pages/miscarriage.aspx.

7. https://www.goodreads.com/author/quotes